LAUS DEO

Almighty God,
you have made us for yourself,
and our hearts are restless
till they find their rest in you.
Teach us to offer ourselves to your service,
that here we may have your peace,
and in the world to come may see you face to face;
through Jesus Christ our Lord.

Collect for Pentecost 18, Alternative Service Book, 1980

THE

RESTLESS HEART

THE LIFE AND INFLUENCE
OF ST. AUGUSTINE

by

MICHAEL MARSHALL

WILLIAM B. EERDMANS PUBLISHING COMPANY
GRAND RAPIDS, MICHIGAN

Dedicated to
BARRY CUMBERLAND
in thanksgiving to God for
his conversion and baptism
into Jesus Christ

Library of Congress Cataloging-in-Publication Data:

Marshall, Michael, 1936–
The restless heart.

Bibliography: p. 151
1. Augustine, Saint, Bishop of Hippo.   2. Christian
saints—Algeria—Hippo—Biography.   3. Hippo (Algeria)—
Biography.   I. Title.
BR1720.A9M337 1987   270.2′092′4 [B]   87-5313

ISBN 0-8028-3632-1

CONTENTS

ACKNOWLEDGMENTS

EVERY writer and speaker is a sort of intellectual jackdaw, continuously attracted by the bright and glittering words and ideas of others. He gives the impression of impertinence as he gathers from all sorts of places, hoarding what he has collected in the nest and then producing it at various moments in books, letters, over the dinner table, or in preaching and teaching. He is an entrepreneur, but hopefully in the sense of the wise scribe, bringing out of his treasure "things new and old." The scholar will spot many phrases, insights, and quotations that have been lifted (and I hope duly acknowledged) from all kinds of sources in the following pages.

Primarily I want to confess and acknowledge a huge debt to Peter Brown's definitive and attractive biography of St. Augustine, to which I return again and again in these pages and at other times. But there are also many other sources, some of which I have remembered and acknowledged and some which I cannot remember because they have now become so much a part of my own thinking. The short bibliography at the back of the book lists some of the books that I have used in my research and that I think could make useful further reading if this volume fires the imagination of its readers to follow the trail.

Then there is the need to acknowledge with deep gratitude the friendship and patience of the Reverend Charles Bewick, who faithfully followed me to the Mediterranean, almost to the Sahara, and up to the Italian Alps, chasing after my obses-

sion with one of the early fathers of the Western church. This book would have been impossible without his outstanding work in taking the remarkable photographs reproduced in these pages. They open up a whole visual world that will hopefully invade our imaginations far more than a merely verbal and printed record ever could. These photographs and illustrations will be a lasting memorial to his visual skills and perceptions. This book is a tangible sacramental of our friendship over many years during which we have worked together in the ministry of the gospel of Jesus Christ.

Mr. Sam Eerdmans went beyond the bounds of professional duty at every point in the production and publication of this book. He encouraged me to complete the book by taking a lively interest in the whole project from the outset.

The "wordsmith" in this whole enterprise has been nothing less than a kind of latter-day Monica—Georgia Streett—who fed all these words into a computer and patiently and swiftly undertook endless corrections and different draftings in the production of the manuscript.

My thanks also are due to Sally Barrett, who strongly encouraged me throughout the days and hours of writing involved in such a work. Furthermore, she undertook the laborious task of editing the manuscript and proofreading it. To all these people and to many others whose names do not readily come to mind I want to acknowledge a deep debt of gratitude.

INTRODUCTION

This book is not a book for scholars, and it is certainly not written by an author who makes any claims to scholarship. Augustine studies constitute a very well-plowed field, and it is doubtful whether there is need (let alone a market) for yet another full-scale book on the life of St. Augustine of Hippo.

However, this book is distinctive in several ways. In the first place, it is the creation of an unapologetic enthusiast. I was given for my birthday in 1972 a copy of Peter Brown's definitive biography, *Augustine of Hippo.* I had studied theology, been through seminary, and worked in the ordained ministry for twelve years. Yet to me the name of Augustine conjured up at that time little more than much of the popular prejudice that is so current about him. As a student of history I had been compelled to read selected passages from the *City of God* and frankly found them somewhat tedious. I knew he was anti-Pelagian and that the Reformers had borrowed heavily from him—that Calvin in particular had gone somewhat overboard for him.

Yet, Peter Brown's biography fired me and set me off with what can only be called a passion for the saint. Since 1972, Augustine has become for me a passion, a hobby, and an enthusiasm bordering on an obsession. Wherever I traveled I collected books about him and as many of his own writings as were in print and accessible.

Then in 1985, under the generous sponsorship of the Anglican Institute, I was able to fulfill an ambition: I was able to undertake a pilgrimage in the steps of St. Augustine. Happily, I was accompanied by my assistant priest, the Reverend Charles Bewick, who has a complementary enthusiasm and hobby (also bordering on an obsession): he is a first-rate amateur photographer. We visited, complete with cameras and much film, the African sites of Hippo, Thagaste, Timgad, and Djemila. From there we went to Rome, from Rome to Milan, and from Milan to Cassago Brianza. Other places in Italy demanded our photographic attention, including Florence. However, for both of us, with our different enthusiasms, the pilgrimage reached its climax in the church of San Pietro Ciel D'oro at Pavia, where the mortal remains of Augustine have been buried under the high altar since the eighth century.

The result is that we have in these pages a "first"— that is, the first fully illustrated life of St. Augustine in English.

And that brings us to the second distinctive feature about this biography. It seems to me that scholars have unwittingly hijacked a saint of the church and buried him beneath the dust and debris of much brilliant scholarship. They have in this way silenced him, prevented him from speaking as he should and indeed as he always did—to the man and woman in the pew. His first biographer, Possidius, claimed that "those who gained most from him were those who had been able actually to see and hear him as he spoke in church" (*Life of St. Augustine,* 31). It is my hope that this biography releases Augustine the scholar from scholars, from the eclectic environment of scholarship, and gives him back to the laity so that we can see him at his best— speaking "in church," inflaming the faithful with vision, hope, and love.

Yet it must be freely admitted that Augustine will either irritate you or fascinate you: he will never simply placate you. You will either have a passion for him or you will be infuriated by him. There is very little middle ground with Augustine of Hippo.

I freely and openly confess that for me it is primarily a fascination that has drawn me to study the life and writings of Augustine. I owe Peter Brown a personal debt of gratitude for opening up for me a whole new world—not only with his biography of Augustine but also with his other writings on the whole era of Augustine—the age of the Late Antiquity.

The highest ambition I can have for this book is that it will fire others to read Peter Brown's biography and then go off on their spiritual pilgrimage and come to know and love that great man of God Bishop Augustine. In the neighborhood of North Africa, where today there is precious little left of Augustine's world and even less of his religion, he is still referred to locally as Rumi Kabir—"The Great Christian." It is perhaps ironic that the world of Islam thus recognizes him while many folks in the pews of the Christian churches scarcely know anything about him.

So I offer this book with the specific aim of popularizing and making attractively accessible the character and features of one of the greatest saints in Christian history. What better occasion to do this than during the course of a special year that celebrates his conversion and baptism exactly sixteen hundred years ago? Holy Augustine, pray for us!

MICHAEL MARSHALL
28 August 1986
St. Augustine's Day

CHAPTER ONE

THE EARLY STRUGGLES

The Roman World of Augustine's Day

Our sea" (*mare nostrum*)—that is what they actually had the audacity to call it! For the robust Roman republic of the empire at its peak, the Mediterranean was to become (at least from *their* proud point of view) little more than an extension of a river—their river—the river Tiber. With Rome at the hub of the known universe and with its magnificent port of Ostia as the point of intersection for all the trade routes of the Mediterranean, why should not the great empire of Rome extend its tentacles to all four points of the compass and so focus prosperity, peace, power, and the pursuit of culture?

Over the centuries of Roman imperialism, however, races and people were to protest and rebel against such a view of the world—and perhaps nowhere quite so conspicuously as in North Africa, which was regarded (again, from a Roman viewpoint) as little more than the granary of Rome tucked away in the provinces of the southern Mediterranean. It had taken the long and bloody Punic wars (three in all, lasting nearly thirty years) finally to subdue what were to become the invaluable provinces of Africa. Divided into three provinces, stretching from what is now Morocco in the west to Libya in the east, the prizes of all the Punic wars proved to be submission of prosperous territory indeed for Rome in the boom period of the empire. In fact, since the conclusion of those Punic wars in 146 B.C., the whole huge area of what constitutes four countries today was entirely within the grasp of the Roman Empire. Mauretania was the name of the Roman province covering Morocco and western Algeria with its capital at Caesaria (now Cherihell). Then eastern Algeria and western Tunisia were bunched together in the province of Numidia with its capital at Cirta (Constantine in contemporary Algeria). The rest—extreme eastern Tunisia and Libya—was the original Roman province of Africa proper, with its capital and port at Carthage (now a suburb of twentieth-century Tunis).

Some such historical background is obviously necessary in our biographical study, because a subtle ingredient in all biography (though perhaps not quite so obvious at first) is the place of climate and the ingredients of geography. It is true of course that the interaction between climate and geography and the human personality has never emerged as a precise science, but few would wish to deny categorically that mankind and its natural habitat do not interact upon each other or that there is absolutely no value whatever in relating the profile of human features to the face of the earth and the colors of the terrain where those features were first formed.

Africa—the Land of Fire and Sun

Our story begins in a part of the world where the coloring is most distinctive, where the contrasts are stark and evident, and where climate and environment alike lend themselves to passion, energy, and the full-blooded rituals of daily life and combat. Furthermore, many of the characteristics of geography and climate (unlike those of history) remain constant over thousands of years and so serve to entice both the historian and the biographer—or better still the pilgrim—to draw very close to the echoes of the voices of those very characters we would wish to study from earlier ages.

Roadsign outside Souk Ahras, known in the days of the Roman Empire as Thagaste, the birthplace of Augustine

In a sense, Augustine of Hippo (as history has come to know him, in order to distinguish him from that other, later Augustine of Canterbury) was essentially a child of North Africa, or, to be more precise, the province of Numidia as it was then called. He was born in the country lodged between the Mediterranean in the north and the huge Sahara Desert in the south—sea and desert constituting equally definitive and hostile boundaries.

The contemporary pilgrim bent upon following in the footsteps of our famous saint (and in a sense that is the only real way to come to know the saints—by seeking to walk in their footsteps) will probably have to fly to the port of Annaba on the north coast of Algeria and then drive (or take the train) sixty miles to Souk Ahras. For that is where the story begins—the birthplace of Augustine— Souk Ahras, or Thagaste as it was called in the Latin tongue of its Roman conquerors. As today, Thagaste was on an elevation of some two thousand feet, and it would experience, as it still does, the contrast between the heat of an African summer and the snow (often deep) of short, sharp, cold winters. The young boy Augustine experienced in his home town four distinct seasons, colorful with wonderful contrasts of land formations, a countryside richly populated (as today) with beautiful wild flowers where energetic birds in the thousands often erupt on being disturbed into a cloudless sky. Storks often dominate the skyline, frequently presiding from their nests, which are proudly built on any convenient and conspicuous promontory, chimney, tower, or turret.

The drive from Annaba to Souk Ahras takes one through country rich in natural deposits of lead and zinc toward country teaming with equally rich veg-etation. Of course such a journey is no long distance by contemporary transport, but for a provincial boy such as Augustine at the beginning of his life, the agricultural life of inland Numidia might have been like that of another planet in distance and distinction from the navigation and trade of the Mediterranean Sea as observed from Annaba. Annaba, or Hippo, where the aging, famous, scholarly, and saintly bishop was to spend many years at the end of his life, is still today the most important city in northern Algeria. As Augustine was to write later in one of his countless letters, "We who were born and brought up among Mediterranean peoples were able, even as children, to imagine the sea from seeing water in a small cup" (*Epistolae*, 7.3.6).

The Provincial Boy

No veneer of schooling, rhetoric, or travel in later life would ever disguise the fact that this Augustine was Punic by his dialect and accent. Even when he was striding the corridors of power at the very center of the empire in Rome and Milan as a successful orator, he was still essentially provincial in his background. His life began in North Africa and ended in North Africa—all in a comparatively small and provincial compass of territory. After all, who has ever heard of Hippo? It was not Hippo that was to make this Augustine important and well known; it was the other way around: the only reason we now remember and recognize Hippo at all is because of Augustine, the saint, the bishop and advocate of full-blooded, orthodox Christianity.

But back to the beginning. Sadly, there is little left for the modern pilgrim to see of Augustine in contemporary Souk Ahras (Thagaste), where today there is a large mosque built over the site of the nineteenth-century church of the days of the French empire. If you can persuade them or make them understand, locals will show you what they like to call Augustine's tree—poor and inadequate evidence of that great local boy who made good. Moslems of Algeria today will probably be more enthusiastic to remind contemporary visitors that it was in this territory that Albert Camus was born in 1913 than to relate to the visitor with any pride that it is where Augustine of Hippo was born A.D. 354.

Yet it was here in Thagaste (to revert to the nomenclature of the fourth-century Roman Empire) on Sunday, November 13, 354, that Aurelius Augustinus, the second son and possibly third child of Patricius Herculus and Monica, his wife, was born. Here, in a city that already had three hundred years of history, was born one who would grow to be a religious genius of the Christian church. His mind and writings not only influenced extensively the church of his day, but later history has proved him to be made of such sturdy and enduring fiber that, after St. Paul, it has to be Augustine of Hippo who has emerged over many centuries as the most formative theologian in the Western world. He is a theological hero for both Protestant and Catholic Christians.

"He that is born in the fire will not melt in the sun" is an old and apt African proverb that might well apply to our Augustine. The searching heat and the sunlight of critical thought and history over the centuries since his day have done little to detract from or to melt down the sturdy substance of his thought; it remains as challenging and enduring as the day its author first committed it to paper.

On the landscape of Western political, philosophical, and religious thought, the seed sown first at Thagaste has blossomed into a fruit that is lastingly significant, that has not been ignored by any serious scholar since Augustine's day. For through his prolific writings, Augustine can still address the issues of our society, our faith, and our prejudices as the second millennium draws to a close almost to the same extent he addressed the issues of the unsettled and turbulent times in which he himself lived.

The Decline of Empire

THE times of Augustine (A.D. 354 to 430) span the ultimate years of decline of one of the most ingenious, vigorous, and productive empires in the history of our world. When Augustine was born, it was not unreasonable to suppose that the rule of mighty Rome would last, if not for a thousand years, then at least to the end of any foreseeable timespan of human imagination. Yet, by the time of his death, only some seventy-six years later, the empire that as a boy at Thagaste he would have taken for granted had crumbled and disintegrated out of all recognition.

Of course, it is true that with the advantage of

Steps in the huge amphitheater of El-Djem in Tunisia

This arch, dating from the days of Augustine, still stands in the city of Djemila, a testimony to the vitality of the civilization that constructed it.

hindsight it is all too easy to identify obvious seeds and signs of decay at work in Roman society many years before Augustine was born. Certainly many of those signs were already clearly in evidence in the life and society of North Africa when Augustine was growing up. The economic expansion and development that had been characteristic of the hinterland of North Africa in the first and second centuries had suddenly come to a halt in the whole of the area we now know as Algeria and Tunisia. And yet not long before Augustine's day, Rome had achieved nothing short of an economic miracle with a chain of fortresses and fortress towns, extensive cultivation, and all the hallmarks of its brilliant and distinctive civilization extending right down to the very edges of the resilient desert of the Sahara.

The modern tourist can still visit the huge amphitheater of El-Djem in Tunisia—a proud statement in stone and strength competing without any apologies in size with nothing less than the great Colosseum at Rome. To this day one can visit the city of Djemila and see the sort of robust life that characterized Roman North Africa in the first centuries. Such a visit strikes the imagination with the realization that in the times of Augustine, this province of the crumbling empire was by no means just a backyard affair. The sturdy columns, many of them still standing, bear testimony to a large city by any standards, carrying all the hallmarks of a healthy and sturdy civilization. Visit Timgad, built A.D. 100 at the orders of Trajan by the soldiers of the great third legion. It is a town only some eighty miles south of Thagaste. As you walk down its streets, which are well preserved by the dry heat and sand, it will not be long before you will capture some glimpse of a society that had flourished and

of a city life that would compare well in its amenities with any sizable city in the ancient world. Like many cities in Africa in the age of the Late Antiquity, Thagaste enjoyed times of prosperity and pleasure wonderfully summarized on a recently discovered memorial stone: "The hunt, the baths, play, and laughter: that's the life for me."

Nevertheless, once decline sets in, history insists that the fall of empires is both rapid and irreversible. Historians have busied themselves over the centuries analyzing the ingredients that make for the rise and fall of cultures and empires. Suffice it to say that by the time of Augustine's boyhood (the second half of the fourth century) all the ingredients and signs were well in evidence for those with eyes to see such sick and sinister indications. The boom period was over; the salad days were at an end. In fact from the very dawn of the fourth century the writing was on the walls of such cities as El-Djem, Djemila, Timgad, and even in Rome itself. In one year—A.D. 307—no fewer than six emperors had occupied the seat of power, ironically resembling in the game of politics something not unlike musical chairs.

For power and politics had indeed become a bit of a game throughout the empire. It was the principal preoccupation of the generals of the ever-larger mercenary armies required to enforce law and order throughout an empire that had grown fat and now sprawled over two and a half million square miles. The emperors, while afforded more and more lavish and outrageous titles of power and authority, promulgating edicts written in gold on purple paper, and handled of course with increasingly abject decorum, were in practice little more than puppets in the hands of the entrepreneurs of political, economic, and military power— in a word the generals. Yes, the writing was most certainly on the wall, and the end of an era of empire was clearly in evidence by the beginning of the fourth century.

Yet decline and decadence originate in the

The road from Madaura, running through a land bounded by the Mediterranean to the north and the Sahara to the south

The amphitheater in El Djem

Above left, *a temple in Djemila*

Above right, *a stork at sunset, a common sight in Augustine's day as now*

Below, *the remains of houses in Timgad*

The fourth-century Bible scholar St. Jerome wrote of his forebodings concerning the disintegration of the Roman Empire.

depths of the human spirit, for men and nations as well as for empires. And truth to tell, the Romans themselves no longer believed in the greatness of Rome. By the fourth century, even the Roman leaders do not seem to have believed in the greatness of anything—not even in the greatness of the great. There was a weariness, a retreat from involvement and responsibility, and an unwillingness to contest any longer for those values, insights, and responsibilities that alone are capable of etching greatness into the mettle of the human spirit. By Augustine's day, decline was evident not only in the plumbing that was ceasing to work and the roads that were no longer being kept in repair. Those are but the outward signs, like the lines on a man's face—evident and clear for all to see. But for the sensitive, robust spirits, the visionaries, the prophets and scholars, there were the inner signs of a crumbling of the whole human spirit, and it was these signs that gave a bleak prognosis for the future—for children and grandchildren.

St. Jerome (ca. 342-420), that craggy, somewhat ill-tempered biblical scholar of the fourth century, wrote about such times of disintegration in a letter concerning a small child, Pacatula, and of the age in which she was to grow up. He writes with a fatalism and a fear for what is coming on the earth. "In such a world, Pacatula has been born. Disaster surrounds her as she plays. She will know of weeping before laughter. . . . She forgets the past; she flees the present, she awaits with eagerness the life to come" (*Epistolae,* 128.5).

It would seem that the millennium neurosis and nuclear forebodings of our own day have been around long before in various keys. There is indeed little if anything that is new under the sun. And, today, in such a climate of despondency and fatalism, humankind seeks every opportunity to flee—if not to the secrecy of the hills, then at least to the security of alternative worlds, worlds that cannot be invaded by everyday responsibilities or be called to account by intellectual or moral demands. In

Augustine's day, as in our own times, there was a fleeing from the world of matter to the conveniently remote world of the spirit, from the world of communication with all its hazards to the so-called inner world with its opportunities for personal, spiritual communion.

The world of the spirit will always be sought in such an age with a new urgency as it promises gently to massage away the irritations and frustrations of the material world of politics and economics and the responsibilities of everyday life. Religion will become primarily a therapy, seldom concerned with the right ordering of everyday life. Religion, like drugs and alcohol, has its addicts and its abusers. So it will not be long before there will be almost two worlds, a schizoid breakdown between the motivating, emerging inner life of the spirit and the necessarily tedious details of the outer life of society. Weariness and indulgence will chase after each other and all this in a climate in which religion, sorcery, superstition, and a phony spiritualism are offering a supermarket of alternative entertainments.

Boyhood and Family

IT was into such a world that not only Pacatula was born but also the young Augustine. He grew up with his elder brother, Navigius, and his sister (whom tradition names Perpetua) in the farmlands of Numidia in the town of Thagaste. We know that Augustine loved to hunt birds: he tells us so. He also tells us that he and his family often had to go about poorly dressed. But what other features can we properly begin to picture in our minds about the young Augustine from what

he tells us about himself and the world in which he lived?

We know that many of the people who lived in Thagaste were of Berber origin—that ancient race of North Africa with swarthy skin. You can still see Berbers to this day, living largely as shepherds and farmers in the Atlas mountains. Warren Thomas Smith describes them as a people of "short stature, of dark complexion, wide shoulders, narrow hips, of nervous personality and energetic temperament" (*Augustine: His Life and Thought*, p. 9). We know from the physical remains of Augustine as a man (both at Hippo, which boasts the relic of his right forearm, and at Pavia, which houses the bones of the rest of his body) that he was short in stature. It might not therefore be wholly inaccurate to borrow the description of a Berber given above and apply it to our saint with respect not only to his personal appearance but even to some extent to his personality.

Schooling—Some Painful Lessons

WE know that as a boy Augustine was precocious, self-conscious, yet bright and quick to grasp and master the things his somewhat erratic will chose to master. For example, he was good at Latin ("I loved Latin" he was to write in later years [*Conf.*, 1.13]); but it seems he was not as good at Greek, for he was frequently beaten for his ineptitude in this subject as a schoolboy.

Already as a young boy, Augustine learned the kind of "prayer" that is common to believers, agnostics, and atheists alike—the prayer of last resort, wrung from us by fear and dismay. "I was still a boy when I first began to pray to you, my Help and Refuge," he was to write many years later. "I used to prattle away to you, and though I was small, my devotion was great when I begged you not to let me be beaten at school. Sometimes, for my own good, you did not grant my prayer, and then my elders and even my parents, who certainly wished me no harm, would laugh at the beating I got—and in those days beatings were my one great bugbear. . . . For, we feared the whip just as much as others fear the rack, and we, no less than they, begged you to preserve us from it" (*Conf.*, 1.9).

Indeed, some of the apprehension of this approaching sadness is reflected in a wonderfully descriptive Renaissance fresco of the young Augustine being taken by his mother, Monica, for his first day at school, only to be greeted by the sight of another young child being beaten. Doubtless the shape of things to come! It was to be (even in the memory of the older Augustine) "a period of suffering and humiliation. I was told that it was right and proper for me as a boy to pay attention to my teachers, so that I should do well at my study of grammar and get on in the world" (*Conf.*, 1.9). In a family where this world's goods are limited and poverty is never very far away, education has often been sold to children as their one chance to get on in the world. We would not be far wrong if we assumed this kind of motivation to have been present in the family of Patricius, Monica, and their able yet quixotic son Augustine. Indeed, they were apparently adamant on this score. "This was the way to gain the respect of others and win for myself what passes for wealth in this world," reports Augustine. "So I was sent to school" (*Conf.*, 1.9).

Monica—Mother and Saint

IN general, Augustine was above average intelligence, and it was presumably not difficult to see, even at an early age, that a scholarly career was within his capabilities if only his father Patricius could find the money for his education. Frankly, it is hard to get a fair picture of Augustine's father. He may have been neither much better nor much worse than most fathers or husbands in Thagaste. Nevertheless, it is his sad lot in history to be on the same stage and playing in the same drama (at least in the early scenes) as the mighty Monica, his wife (cast as no less than a mother and saint in her own right). Inevitably in that quality of casting, he will be upstaged at every turn of the drama. Augustine, our only source for information on Patricius, has very little to say about his father precisely because he has so very much to say about his mother. So we have to take her first, because she is of first importance in the formation of her famous son.

"She had the weak body of a woman but the strong faith of a man, the composure of her years, a mother's love for her son, and the devotion of a Christian" (*Conf.*, 9.4). There is enough of substance per square inch in that commendation to render a second parent's contribution almost redundant. Augustine writes at length in later years of the virtues of his mother, and the church throughout the centuries has taken up the accolade and honored her as a saint (with her own day in the church's calendar—May 4). For her son, who became so famous and formative in the history of the church, was converted to Christianity in large measure in answer to her prayers and tears over thirty-three years. Furthermore, as though the conversion of her son were not enough, Augustine himself is at pains to let us all know that she had previously been largely responsible (through additional prayers and tears) for the conversion of Patricius, her somewhat wayward husband: "In the end she won her husband . . . as a convert in the very last days of his life on earth" (*Conf.*, 9.9). It is a truly impressive record.

Surely we could be forgiven in a post-Freudian age for seeing some destructive aspects in such an overbearing mother figure who frankly pursued Augustine, not unlike the Hound of Heaven, down the corridors of the first thirty-three years of his life. Augustine's own eulogy for his mother (again admittedly written in later and more mature years) appears to be almost unqualified. "In the flesh," Augustine is concerned to remind us, "she brought me to birth in this world: in her heart she brought me to birth in your eternal light" (*Conf.*, 9.8).

Yet there are—because frankly there need to be—redeeming features in all assessments of sanctity. Augustine's assessment of his mother is no exception to this rule. His eulogy for her differs markedly from post-Christian assessments of personality and biography in at least two important respects. We need to note them at this early stage for they are recurring themes that are much more powerfully orchestrated in Augustine's later theological works.

In the first place, sanctity, in Augustine's book, is never based upon self-acquired virtues or natural talents and strengths. It is always God's gift—received and not achieved, the direct result of God's amazing grace. It is amazing grace and grace alone for which Augustine will contend without apology in his later heady theological contests against such heretics and schismatics as the Donatists and the Pelagians. He writes of his mother's virtues in the same way that he wishes us to perceive his own gifts and the gifts of all God's saints. "It is not of her gifts that I shall speak, but of the gifts you gave to her. For she was neither her own maker nor her own teacher. It was you who made her. . . . It was by Christ's teaching, by the guidance of your only Son, that she was brought up to honour and obey you in one of those good Christian families which form the body of your Church" (*Conf.*, 9.8). Virtue for Augustine from first to last is a gift. Because it is freely given, it is less likely to prove a tyrant or be so destructive as the virtues of self-made and secular-minded men and women.

Second, the sanctity with which Augustine was concerned and for which he strove all his life after his baptism and conversion at the age of thirty-three is characterized as that uniquely Christian strength that is never ashamed to tell us in the same breath of its weakness. Indeed, it is in the very weakness itself that the strength is best discerned and discovered. Such a view of sanctity willingly delights to sketch the portrait of the saint with warts and all. It sees irony and comedy at the heart of all true holiness (almost like that of a good joke) and refutes any attempt at self-justification, which is inevitably founded upon the quicksand of good works or, even worse, upon a good reputation. Rather, such good works (however impressive) are always built upon the rock of a lively faith as robust in weakness and defeat as in strength and victory.

Clearly there was something of a family legend surrounding Monica. It is obvious that from the outset she had enjoyed with her own family something of a "saintly" reputation. Yet we can rejoice that her sanctity had also become something of a family joke. Perhaps the story, like all good stories, became embroidered with the telling. Possibly it arose out of a need within the family to cope with Monica, whose life so clearly bore the fruits of the spirit in such remarkable though at times rather overbearing ways. However, the story stood in the family memory and was frequently told of how, even at an early age, she nearly became a tippler.

It appears that as a young child, Monica "developed a secret liking for wine. Her parents, believing her to be a good and obedient child, used to send her to draw wine from the cask, as was the custom. She used to dip the cup through the opening at the top of the barrel, and before pouring the wine in the flagon she would sip a few drops. . . . Each day she added a few more drops to her daily sip of wine. . . . It soon became a habit." Happily the young girl did not grow up into an alcoholic, for we are told in the completion of the family story, which as we might suspect had a happy ending, that Monica "used to go to the cellar with a servant-girl. One day when they were alone, this girl quarrelled with her young mistress, as servants do, and intending it as a most bitter insult, called [the young Monica] a drunkard." Clearly "the word struck home," Augustine tells us, as doubtless Monica had frequently told him in lessons learned at her knee from an early age. For at once Monica "condemned it and renounced it" (*Conf.,* 9.8). She was not to be a tippler after all!

Patricius—a Faint-hearted Father

For every sentence of this story and so many more that Augustine delighted to tell of his mother, there is scarcely a single word about his father, who we are told blatantly was unfaithful to his wife, sullen, and given to bouts of anger and aggression. The little that Augustine does choose to tell us is strangely inappropriate and implies alienation and a lack of trust between the growing son and his father. "One day at the public baths he [Patricius] saw the signs of active virility coming to life" in his son. "He was happy to tell" Monica about it (*Conf.,* 2.3), but we might suspect reluctant and awkward perhaps in trying to share with an adolescent son some of the responsibilities and pitfalls of his developing sexuality.

However, Augustine does make some positive comments about his father. "No one had anything but praise for my father who, despite his slender resources, was ready to provide his son with all that was needed to enable him" to receive a good education. Augustine took pains to point out that "Many of our townsmen, far richer than my father, went to no such trouble for their children's sake" (*Conf.,* 2.3). Monica and Patricius, divided though they were on some things, were united in one main objective concerning their growing son. Both of them, Augustine tells us, were ambitious for him to achieve distinction in his studies—a distinction that would lead to wealth, status, and opportunities to break out of the small world of Thagaste. "Both my parents" he records with restrained approval "were unduly eager for me to learn" (*Conf.,* 2.3).

In fact, the young Augustine was rapidly outgrowing the mold of any schooling that could be afforded for him at Thagaste. It was not long before his ambitious father was determined that his able fifteen-year-old son should go some twenty miles away for continued and further schooling—to Madaura.

A street in Madaura, the city in which the fifteen-year-old Augustine received formal education, principally in the field of "literature and the art of public speaking"

Madaura—Away at School

MADAURA was a city already famous for its schooling and for being the home of the renowned second-century writer, orator, and platonist Apuleius, celebrated author of *The Golden Ass.* Apuleius of Madaura was literally a name to conjure with in Augustine's day as an author of many books that mixed magic, religion, and sex together. He also wrote more serious and lengthy tomes on platonic philosophy.

But back to Madaura. Here was a city that boasted the statues and temples of the pagan gods at every street corner. The ruins of the Christian basilica are visible there to this day, yet the church in that city, as in so many cities of the Roman Empire in the fourth century, still contested against the sturdy and stubborn superstitions of paganism. The trappings of paganism were still clearly in evidence long after the Peace of Constantine, some forty years before Augustine's birth, and they were slow to die.

Since A.D. 313, Christianity had been the official and accepted though by no means the exclusive religion of the Roman Empire. Hard by the Christian basilicas in all cities of the empire in Augustine's day there were ornate and robust temples of the pagan gods. In the city squares it was the pagan temples and not the Christian churches that were most impressive and most in evidence, with their proud columns and their impressive porticos lending splendor and grandeur to the public life of politics and the marketplace. Constantine had long since said of the Christian symbol of the cross that "In this sign we conquer"—but that sign and its accompanying faith had by no means conquered the skylines of the cities or the hearts of their

Above, *the remains of thermae (private baths) in Madaura*
Below, *a mural by Bernozzo Gozzoli depicting Augustine at school*

Above, *a view of the forum in Madaura*
Left, *a shepherd in the fields near Madaura*

citizens in the Roman Empire of the fourth century.

So it was with the young Augustine. At fifteen he had not yet been baptized. He was "blessed regularly from birth with the sign of the Cross and was seasoned with God's salt" (*Conf.*, 1.11)—salt placed on the tongue. Although as a child, when suddenly taken ill, he had begged his mother to arrange for him to be baptized, Monica had held out against this, for in such an age and in such a world, baptism was regarded as the great divide between the world of paganism and the new life of Christian discipleship. It is true that if the little boy Augustine had drawn very close to death, Monica "would have hastened to see that [he] was admitted to the sacraments of salvation and washed clean. . . . for the pardon of [his] sins" (*Conf.*, 1.11). But Christianity was in evidence in Madaura as in the rest of the world of Late Antiquity, contesting for its survival and its faith amid a plethora of religious options and philosophical alternatives. To all of this the young Augustine would be fully exposed for the first time when he went away from home (admittedly only twenty miles away) to school in Madaura.

The school at Madaura, we are told, was little more than a large hut, possibly divided from the noisy street outside by a curtain. Fees—albeit modest—had to be paid for such schooling to a schoolmaster, whose profession in those days was clearly defined (as in later tradition) by distinctive dress.

In his spiritual autobiography—the *Confessions*—Augustine tells us that the main emphasis in the education he received in Madaura was in the field of "literature and the art of public speaking" (*Conf.*, 2.3). Of course the world of the Late Antiquity was densely populated with great literary figures such as Cicero, Sallust, Virgil, and Terence—the "idol of Africa," who had been born in Carthage. In fact, Rome and Africa could boast a whole galaxy of distinguished writers. It would almost seem that there was something about the climate or the expectations of Africa that called out wordsmiths of both the written and the spoken variety.

With the benefit of hindsight, we can now see how the well-known fathers of the church (Cyprian, Tertullian, and of course St. Augustine), conspicuous for their spoken and written words, belonged to a larger environment of secular writers and rhetoricians. For example, there was Manilius of the first century, who had written a handbook on astrology—in verse as an added attraction. Then there was Fronto of the second century, who had achieved the dizzy heights of being appointed as tutor to the emperor Marcus Aurelius. Aulus Gellius could also claim some place in this cast of stars as author of the *Attic Nights*, what Henry Chadwick delightfully calls "a kind of reader's digest to effective dinner party conversation" (*Augustine*, p. 5).

It was the impact of such pagan writings that produced and formed the world of classical mythology. Such mythology in its turn also populated man's view of the universe with the drama of the gods and demigods—a sort of supernatural soap opera or its equivalent in today's science fiction—strongly colored with lurid, sensual, and erotic escapades. Once the pupil had mastered the maps of this mythology, he could have at his fingertips a rich and seductive vocabulary of legends, myths, and analogies—the stock in trade of any public speaker of Augustine's day.

And, as we might expect, Augustine was sharp to master this syllabus. By an early age he had the whole repertoire at his fingertips—or perhaps we should say on the tip of his tongue. But he does not hesitate to tell us at this time (at the young age of sixteen) that he felt himself no longer in the life of the church: "frenzy gripped me and I surrendered myself entirely to lust" (*Conf.*, 2.2).

A Setback: Thagaste

It was especially unfortunate, therefore, that once having broken loose from the small-town life of Thagaste, and sensing the wider opportunities afforded to him by the environment at Madaura, Augustine should be recalled again to his hometown of Thagaste after little less than a year away because of the lack of money to pay for his fees. He was obliged to "leave school and live idly at home" with his parents (*Conf.*, 2.3).

The return could not have come at a worse moment. "The brambles of lust grew high above my head," he tells us, "and there was no one to root them out, certainly not my father" (*Conf.*, 2.3). The boy Augustine was daily growing into a young man with drives and passions that needed direction and purpose. At home there was clearly little to stretch him, and soured boredom soon turned to foolish and fruitless frivolities. He spent his days at the public baths and the rest of his time with a band of local youths, equally bored and vying with each other in lawlessness, vandalism, and vice. He tells us that when he was with these companions he "was ashamed to be less dissolute than they were" (*Conf.*, 2.3). He reports, "I heard them bragging of their depravity, and the greater the sin the more

they gloried in it, so that I took pleasure in the same vices, not only for the enjoyment of what I did, but also for the applause I won." In fact, it pleased him to "rival other sinners." He writes, "I used to pretend that I had done things I had not done at all, because I was afraid that innocence would be taken for cowardice and chastity for weakness" (*Conf.*, 2.3). There must be few human beings who have not known that situation, but perhaps not quite so many who would be willing to admit it. Clearly it was this kind of motivation that led him headlong into the famous incident with the stolen pears and the pear tree.

"There was a pear-tree near our vineyard, loaded with fruit that was attractive neither to look at nor to taste. Late one night," playing out of doors until well after dark, "a band of ruffians" including the young Augustine, age sixteen, "went off to shake down the fruit and carry it away. . . . We took away an enormous quantity of pears, not to eat them ourselves, but simply to throw them to the pigs. Perhaps we ate some of them, but our real pleasure consisted in doing something that was forbidden" (*Conf.*, 2.4).

It is at this point in the *Confessions* that we begin to taste something of the quality of the ultimate record of his life—a record that Augustine willingly and humbly shares with his readers. For the real world for Augustine is always the interior world of human motivation; the most important moral conflict does not lie so much in externals as in the interior and frequently inaccessible and hidden recesses of our hearts and wills. At times (especially in the *Confessions*) it is as though our saint has stepped right out of the fourth-century world and is out of sequence with history. It would seem that he is addressing us in post-Freudian language and with features of Renaissance self-awareness. He tells us that he had no wish "to enjoy things" he had stolen but only "to enjoy the theft" for its own sake. Apparently he had no need of the pears. He did not need to steal them in order to satisfy hunger. Clearly there was no rational motivation that can be deduced. So he bids us look unsparingly into the heart, to tell us "what prompted" his actions.

"Look into my heart, O God, the same heart on which you took pity when it was in the depths of the abyss. Let my heart now tell you what prompted me to do wrong for no purpose, and why it was only my own love of mischief that made me do it" (*Conf.*, 2.4). He is not looking as modern man so often does at external circumstances or for an explanation that will excuse or ameliorate the deed and its consequences. There is no turning here to genes, environment, cultural conditioning, or even to the stars. On the contrary, he concludes his searching and penetrating self-analysis with the bald statement that he enjoyed "doing wrong for no other reason than that it was wrong" (*Conf.*, 2.6).

He "relished and enjoyed" stealing those pears for no other reason than to satisfy a desire to steal them. It would seem that sin has a power that can be derived solely from the sheer pleasure of committing the sin. For Augustine such actions form the baseline of human depravity. He is under no delusions about the power of sin and evil at work in the life of mankind and in the record of human history. Here is a condition that cannot be remedied merely by education (whether at Madaura, Carthage, Milan, Yale, or Cambridge). Education and self-improvement (however much coveted for him by Patricius or by any well-meaning parent or benefactor) are powerless in themselves to cope with this kind of capacity for self-destruction and

depravity. This theme was to form the basis of his later theological writings and crusades.

Contemporary man, especially before the two world wars and the horrors of contemporary human holocausts, has been tempted to suppose that the human moral dilemma is little more than the result of external forces that underlie human life and human history. Such a mild diagnosis seems to require only a mild palliative: the medium of education and a little environmental spring cleaning from time to time. Sadly, it has taken two world wars, the sophistication of modern human torture, an Auschwitz, and a Buchenwald to remind us of what Augustine never forgot and what in every page of his writings he calls us to remember: mankind is depraved. That is the bad news. But it is not the last word. There is the medicine of salvation, infinitely more potent than education. There is the free gift of God's grace and strength available to all who are willing to plumb the depths of the human problem.

The self-made man always finds this emphasis upon salvation a difficult concept. He is tempted to replace salvation with mere education or a naive belief in automatic growth, development, and progress. This is because he has never consciously been to the edge of the precipice, looked into that abyss of self-destruction (of which Augustine speaks), and known that grace and grace alone has pulled him back, turned him round, and saved him from the destructiveness of his own strengths and talents as well as his weaknesses and failings.

In his introspection, Augustine knew all too well from firsthand experience, travel, and the geography of the human heart the need for salvation through grace. He went frequently to the edges of that precipice and he looked into that abyss. He did

A temple in Djemila

not forget, nor will he let us forget, that humanity is desperate in its need to be rescued. The way to our salvation is through grace and grace alone. In reality the situation for humanity is perilous, and the solution is more likely to be found in the environment of an emergency unit than in the open-ended leisure of mere therapy.

Later theologians and those who have written about Augustine have so often chosen to hear only half of his message. They have deduced from his writings something less than orthodoxy. They would have us believe that to the modern secular mind—and indeed to large parts of the contemporary church (extensively and strangely secularized)—Augustine's language concerning sin is too strong by half. His diagnosis, they contest, is too negative and too pessimistic. Yet we must remember that this is not Augustine's last word any more than it is God's last word. The last word is good news. Problems are solutions in disguise. A realistic diagnosis of mankind's sickness opens up the way to the good news of grace, healing, and salvation. These are the principal themes of his later writings as theologian, bishop, and pastor.

But at sixteen, Augustine was not ready to hear this good news. At that age few are. It was to take another sixteen years or so for him to experience for himself God's strength in his weakness and God's health in his sickness. Then we shall discover an Augustine with good news on his tongue and gladness in his heart.

But at this point in our story and indeed at this point in Augustine's life, "good news" of a different kind was to come from a rather different quarter.

CHAPTER TWO

HEADY DAYS IN CARTHAGE

Carthage

AUGUSTINE had been brought back home from Madaura while Patricius his father, "a modest citizen of Thagaste, whose determination was greater than his means, saved up the money to send" his son "farther afield to Carthage" to complete his education (*Conf.*, 2.3). Yet, happily for Augustine, there lived in Thagaste (that is to say on the rare occasions when business and legal matters did not compel him to be away from home) one Romanianus. We shall be bumping into Romanianus a good deal later in the story, but suffice it to say at this stage that this wealthy and generous patron befriended the young Augustine and as his benefactor paid a large part toward Augustine's education in Carthage. That was good news indeed!

"I went to Carthage, where I found myself in the midst of a hissing cauldron of lust," writes Augustine (*Conf.*, 3.1). So A.D. 371, at the age of seventeen, he arrived in the great seaport town of Carthage, still the second city of the Roman Empire (just outside of Tunis). "I had not yet fallen in love, but I was in love with the idea of it," he freely admitted later. "I began to look around for some object for my love, since I badly wanted to love something. I had no liking for the safe path without pitfalls, for although my real need was for you, my God, who are the food of the soul, I was not aware of this hunger." Instead, "to love and to have my love returned" he confessed in later life, "was my heart's desire, and it would be all the sweeter if I could also enjoy the body of the one who loved me" (*Conf.*, 3.1).

Certainly life in Carthage was to be more exciting than in either Thagaste or Madaura. He was away from his family and friends in general, and in particular he was at last away from Monica—at least for a while, though if prayers are capable of bridging time and distance, then in reality he was never far away from Monica at any point in his life, at least in spirit.

Of course, like all great international seaports, Carthage offered all kinds of opportunities for every kind of lawless and sensual pursuit. The great Roman baths, begun by the emperor Hadrian A.D. 112 and completed by Antoninus Pius about A.D. 146, were among the largest within the whole Roman Empire. You can see the general layout of these Roman baths at Carthage to this day. They were located near the sea and in their day housed large and elaborate heating arrangements. In fact, the ash and cinder used in this sophisticated process are still visible after all these years in the central octagon. A little way from the heating system, in the shade and cool and for use during the hot siesta hours, the large rest rooms in the ground floor are still there for today's tourist to inspect. Here, as elsewhere, the baths were the delight and playground of the empire, not least in its years of decline and decadence.

An Unsafe Path

THERE can be little question that on arriving unmarried in Carthage, Augustine, at least for the first year, did not seek out the safe path. A young man at his age, unless he had been seeking a career at the hands of ambitious parents, as Augustine undoubtedly was, would probably by this time have been anchored within marriage. Not so Augustine: no cautious arrangement for him!

Things had perhaps been made more difficult by the constant "warnings" from Monica "not to commit fornication and above all not to seduce any man's wife" (*Conf.,* 2.3).

"So I muddied the stream of friendship with the filth of lewdness and clouded its clear waters with hell's black river of lust" (*Conf.,* 3.1). In a somewhat belated adolescence, Augustine clearly kicked over the traces, with head on high "cutting a fine figure in the world."

If you did not like "the safe path," there were plenty of other paths to take in fourth-century Roman Carthage. From those huge and somewhat decadent baths of Antoninus by the seashore, turning your back on the harbor ringed with colonnades, it was not a long path to bypass the Christian basilica as you headed toward town past huge and impressive Corinthian-style columns and walked down avenues shaded by trees and past bookstalls that lined the streets in the direction of the temple of Asclepius. Just to your right was the theater. Traveling straight on and perhaps passing children in the street playing hopscotch games ingrained (where they still are) in the stones of the pavement, eventually you would arrive at the huge amphitheater, almost as large as the Colosseum in Rome. (Incidentally, this coliseum was made conspicuous in recent times by the visit of Winston Churchill in 1943 when he addressed the victorious Allied troops from amidst its fallen columns and broken marble.)

A Passion for the Theater

We can be sure, then, that there were plenty of unsafe paths for an energetic, head-strong young man to follow in Carthage in the closing years of the Roman Empire. In this big city, as it turned out, the imaginative Augustine was "much attracted by the theatre" (*Conf.,* 3.2). In the histrionic way of the self-conscious and the young, Augustine adored feeling "sad at the sight of tragedy and suffering on the stage" (*Conf.,* 3.2). Of course for a man for whom words were "cups" and for whom the spoken word was to claim so important a role in life, it is hardly surprising that the drama of the theater should from the outset be so enticing and appealing. It is not difficult to imagine him indulging fully in the life of the theater, as he admits that "in those unhappy days I enjoyed the pangs of sorrow. I always looked for things to wring my heart and the more tears an actor caused me to shed by his performance on the stage, even though he was portraying the imaginary distress of others, the more delightful and attractive I found it" (*Conf.,* 3.2).

All his life, after his conversion, Augustine was suspicious of the theater, and, as bishop of Hippo, he frequently exhorted the faithful to refrain from attending. Indeed, Augustine is frequently quoted by puritans in support of their abhorrence of the theater. Yet in this area as in so many other areas of Augustine's life, if we want to understand him, we must first come to the matter at hand from his direction and starting point, which is probably the very opposite of our own.

Augustine never championed apathy or indifference. He was supremely a man of passion and compassion. His starting point was one of overreaction and too much sympathy. That was his problem. "Of course," he contends in speaking of the theater, "this does not mean that we must arm ourselves against compassion." On the contrary, he

Below, *the amphitheater in Djemila.* "I was much attracted by the theatre," wrote Augustine of his youth. "In those unhappy days I enjoyed the pangs of sorrow. . . . The more tears an actor caused me to shed by his performance on the stage . . . the more delightful and attractive I found it" (Conf., 3.2).

Carthage was a significant city in the Roman Empire, an international seaport. The great Roman baths (left) were among the largest in the empire.

Below, *the KARTHAGE mosaic on the Via della Corporazione in Ostia*

asserts, "there are times when we must welcome sorrow on behalf of others" (*Conf.,* 3.2). Here was a young man who was too easily, too deeply moved to tears and who overidentified with the world around him. He would write with the perspective of later life that "I am not nowadays insensible to pity. But in those days I used to share the joy of stage lovers and their sinful pleasure in each other even though it was all done in make-believe for the sake of entertainment; and when they were parted, pity of a sort led me to share their grief" (*Conf.,* 3.2).

So it was for Augustine, in the whole world of sensual response. His religion, his love, his sexuality, and his aesthetic responses were all white hot. He has little to say to cold apathy or self-righteous indifference. Many years later in his late fifties he was to write these words: "Give me a man in love; he knows what I mean. Give me one who yearns; give me one who is hungry; give me one far away in this desert, who is thirsty and sighs for the spring of the Eternal country. Give me that sort of man: he knows what I mean. But if I speak to a cold man, he just does not know what I am talking about" (*Tract on St. John's Gospel,* 26.4). That is not the writing of a cold man and certainly not the caution of a puritan.

Rather, we have in Augustine a man who lusted with hunger and thirst and whose problem was that he went too far too easily. The "safe path" did not in Carthage lead to the basilica, yet Augustine confesses to God that he even went "so far as to relish the thought of lust, and gratify it too, within the walls of your church during the celebration of your mysteries" (*Conf.,* 3.3).

Modern, apathetic man, sick and in need often of the stimulation today of pornography and other forms of titillation, is coming from the very opposite end of the spectrum from the young Augustine in Carthage. Perhaps, like the "cold man," we do not even know what he is talking about. The voyeurism of apathy needs a very different correction from the correction that Augustine needed in the excesses of his feeling and passion at the age of seventeen in Carthage. He would find much that would puzzle him in our contemporary weariness, indifference, and coldness and would doubtless admonish us today with different instructions from those that he gave in a very different climate and from his own very special perspective.

A Successful Student

YET while all this tension was part of Augustine's experience in the early days in Carthage, "besides these pursuits I was also studying for the law. Such ambition was held to be honourable and I was determined to succeed in it." In fact, by the end of that first year he "was at the top of the school of rhetoric" (*Conf.,* 3.3).

All this, of course, must have been very pleasing to Romanianus. From Augustine's earliest days Romanianus had been a generous and caring benefactor and patron. By any standards Augustine was now clearly "doing well." His father had been unable to afford to pay for a full education; it had been and continued to be Romanianus who had made all this possible. All through his early life (in fact until his conversion) Augustine sought out father figures, heroes, and men whom he could emulate. This explains a succession of older men who played an important and vital role in Augustine's life, from Romanianus to Bishop Ambrose of

Milan, balancing a little perhaps the overriding and rather overbearing influence of Monica, his mother.

So Romanianus would certainly have been pleased with the results of Augustine's first year at Carthage. As an international lawyer, he had led just the kind of life that a provincial and small-town boy like Augustine would most respect and emulate. Back in Thagaste he had been something of a local hero. He spent his life frequently sailing to Italy and to the heart of the empire at the imperial court to defend his property. On his return to the small town of Augustine's birth, he gave wild beast shows and received speeches and praise from his fellow townsmen, among whom in the early days had numbered Augustine's father, Patricius. In all that busy and successful life he had taken a lively interest in the young Augustine and spotted in him something of the protégé. Later in life, Augustine acknowledged freely and generously a debt to Romanianus:

> In my youth when I, a poor boy, was pursuing my studies, you aided me by the hospitality of your home, by paying my expenses, and, what is more, by the encouragement you gave me; you consoled me by your friendship when I was deprived of my father. You inspired me with confidence; you helped me with money; you made me almost as well known, you placed me almost in the same rank as yourself in our town by your good will, your friendship, by sharing your very home with me.
>
> —Contra Academicos, *2.3*

And so, at the top of the school of rhetoric, Augustine felt he had honored the trust and support of his benefactor and patron. He had just the

sort of ambition that struggling self-made men supported by benefactors so frequently display. He freely admits that he was pleased with his "superior status and swollen with conceit." Perhaps it was such vanity that kept him at a distance from some of the terrorizing fraternities—"The Wreckers"—as they were fashionably known. He says, in fact, that he had "nothing whatever to do with their outbursts of violence" although he lived among them and "kept company with them." Part of him wanted to go along with this "set," but he "always had a horror" of what they got up to when "without provocation they would set upon some timid newcomer, gratuitously affronting his sense of decency for their own amusement and using it as fodder for their spiteful jests" (*Conf.,* 3.3). Universities and educational establishments have not changed all that very much over the centuries!

But the overriding dynamic in Augustine's makeup was his "ambition to be a good speaker, for the unhallowed and inane purpose of gratifying human vanity" (*Conf.,* 3.4). He really had identified with the speeches and drama of the stage. There was always to be in him something of the drama of the actor, aided and enhanced by the power of eloquence. Yet, whether it was ambition, some measure of growth and maturity, or the prayers of the mighty Monica back home in Thagaste that led him to do so, in the two years following the first year in Carthage he disciplined his ebullient spirit and began a serious search for truth, making a strong commitment to study and work.

Family Affairs

In fact, from the close of his first year in Carthage, at the age of nineteen, Augustine had a large agenda of concerns that probably more than anything else would help him to "settle down." In the first place there was the death of his father. So far as we know this was sudden and unexpected. He was not an old man at his death. It would not be unreasonable to suppose that Augustine would feel some grief and bereavement on the death of Patricius or that something of this would emerge in his spiritual journal, the *Confessions.* Yet in effect, the death of his father scarcely gets a passing reference. "I was now in my nineteenth year and she [Monica] supported me, because my father had died two years before" (*Conf.,* 3.4). And so it would be Monica who would now take responsibility (not a light one financially or in any other way) for completing her son's education. Of course she would not have wanted it otherwise!

There was, however, something she would most certainly have wished otherwise. For it was also at about this time that Augustine took to himself a concubine. "In those days I lived with a woman, not my lawful wedded wife but a mistress whom I had chosen for no special reason but that my restless passions had alighted on her. But she was the only one and I was faithful to her" (*Conf.,* 4.2). We do not know the name of this girl who lived with Augustine and shared his life for the next fifteen years.

In the world of the late empire, such relationships, although regarded as second-class marriages, were by no means disreputable; they were traditional and honorable features of society in Augustine's day. The church recognized contracts of

this sort, and indeed the relationships were often marked by fidelity from both parties. There is no reason to suppose otherwise with Augustine and his unnamed concubine. After all, why would Augustine at the outset of his career want to be fettered to a wife in formal marriage, with all the responsibilities that accompanied such an arrangement in the society of his day? Ironically, later in life as a celibate bishop preaching to his congregation in Hippo, Augustine has the audacity to forbid others to do precisely what he had done in earlier life (admittedly before his baptism). "If you have no wives, you may not have concubines, women whom you will later dismiss in order to marry a wife" (*Sermons,* 312.2).

As a provincial professor, Augustine had little motivation to be tied in some early match, perhaps to some lower-class family from among the folks back home. Better far to have such an arrangement as he had in Carthage that could quite frankly be dispensed with or painlessly retailored at a later stage to suit his emerging career. Many people of similar status in Augustine's day found a concubine a perfectly respectable arrangement. In fact, although we have to read between the lines to establish some kind of picture of this relationship in Augustine's life, it is clear that he thought highly of her and held her in high respect. When she was dismissed later, this elusive figure in Augustine's life was to leave him "vowing never to know a man again."

Strangely enough, Augustine's concubine appears again for those with eyes to see (including, we may hope, Augustine himself) in long and somewhat tortuous moral advice on marriage he gave in his writings as a bishop. There he tackles the subject head on. This problem often arises, he says, *if a man and a woman live together without being legitimately joined, not to have children, but because they could not observe continence; and if they have agreed between themselves to have relations with no one else, can this be called a marriage? Perhaps: but only if they have resolved to maintain until death the good faith which they had promised themselves. . . . Indeed if a man takes a woman only for a time, until he has found another who better suits his rank and fortune; and if he marries this woman, as being of the same class, this man would commit adultery in his heart, not toward the one whom he had married, but towards her with whom he had lived without being legitimately married. The same can be said for the woman. . . . Nevertheless, if she was faithful to him, and if, after his marriage to another, she herself gave no thought to marriage but abstained from all sexual relations, I would not dare to accuse her of adultery—even though she may have been guilty, in living with a man who was not her husband.*

—De bono coniug., 5.1

So surely Augustine does not wish history to accuse his unnamed concubine of adultery. She probably lived the rest of her life after being dismissed by Augustine as a devout communicant Christian—though not before bearing for Augustine his only son, Adeodatus, A.D. 372. Adeodatus (the name means "God's gift") was very important to Augustine, and although he only lived to be seventeen, we shall find him later in our story beside his father in the last months leading up to his baptism, and indeed we shall find him by his father's side on the day of their baptism in the waters of regeneration in Milan at the hands of its illustrious bishop. The name Adeodatus might on

first hearing sound unduly pretentious. We know, however, that while it also had obvious religious connotations in its Punic form, Iatanbaal, it was a familiar name for a boy in the Carthage of Augustine's day.

But back to Augustine. His father had died. He had been "washed upon the shore of matrimony" or at least an honorable version of it, and he was now the father of a young son. All this within three years of arriving in Carthage.

The Quest for Wisdom

IN fact, however, the journey of the inner life of Augustine at this point was to have far more significance than any of these outward events or traumas. It is the journey of the inner life of Augustine with which we must be primarily concerned, as he was. At the age of nineteen, A.D. 373, the young Augustine passed through the first of many deep, inner, searching experiences. Many years later in his *Confessions*, Augustine pinpoints the age of nineteen as "the age at which I had first begun to search in earnest for truth and wisdom and had promised myself that, once I had found them, I would give up all the vain hopes and mad delusions which sustained my futile ambitions" (*Conf.*, 6.11).

With a restless heart and searching mind, during his third year in Carthage, in "the prescribed course of study" Augustine stumbled upon and was arrested by the work of the great Cicero, and one work particularly—the *Hortensius*. He freely admits that "it altered my outlook on life . . . , provided me with new hopes and aspirations. All my empty dreams suddenly lost their charm and my

Cicero, the great Roman statesman, orator, and philosopher whose works first taught Augustine not simply to study wisdom but to love wisdom

heart began to throb with a bewildering passion for the wisdom of eternal truth. I began to climb out of the depths to which I had sunk" (*Conf.,* 3.4).

So the inner journey began, through philosophy and religion, eventually leading its pilgrim to Christianity. In retrospect, however, Augustine did not speak of his search for God but rather of God's search for him. It was God in and through all the alternatives of philosophy (even superstitions) and religion who was drawing Augustine to himself and ultimately into the arms of the church. The evidence for this searching God is the restless heart. "Where could my heart find refuge from itself?" (*Conf.,* 4.7). He was like a butterfly moving from one option to another in a vast market of religious flowers only to find that each is synthetic; all the blooms have the scent of the real thing, yet each finally proves to be a cheat and a fraud.

The physical geography of Augustine's journey in the next few years was erratic and extensive. After three years as a student at Carthage (A.D. 371-74) he returned to his hometown, Thagaste, to teach rhetoric. Then it was back to Carthage after scarcely a year to pursue his career. From there to Rome and from Rome to Milan. We need to follow the story every step of the way and note the development of the story line at each turning of the road—though again, this is not the most important journey we shall be tracing. Always more significant is the journey and pilgrimage of the heart (that same restless heart) and mind. The turning points on the road are marked by formative books that Augustine picked and read. In the beginning the particular book was Cicero's *Hortensius.* Through that Augustine took the first vital step in the journey of the heart. Many years later and much further down the path, another book would constitute another crucial milestone—the Bible. He would

open that book and read it and find that at last he had come home not to Thagaste but to that place and state where he could finally "rest in God."

But back to Cicero. Augustine opened the *Hortensius* and read it intensely. What he read there spoke to his condition in Carthage and in fact still spoke to him many years later when he was a bishop and writing his great work on the Trinity. "If the souls which we have are eternal and divine, we must conclude that the more we let them have their head in their natural activity, that is, in reasoning and in the quest for knowledge, and the less they are caught up in the vices and errors of mankind, the easier it will be for them to ascend and return to heaven" (*De Trinitate,* 19.26) This was the best Wisdom philosophy of the ancient world, and it spoke eloquently and powerfully to the young Augustine of wisdom and of God. If he could become less "caught up in the vices and errors of mankind," could he not also "ascend and return to heaven"? This was the path to wisdom. Cicero taught Augustine not simply to study wisdom but to love wisdom. "In Greek," he reminds us, "the word 'philosophy' means 'love of wisdom,' and it was with this love that the *Hortensius* inflamed me" (*Conf.,* 3.4). Cicero taught him from the outset not simply "to admire one or other of the schools of philosophy."

Cicero's words inflamed Augustine and set him "burning with fire," but the "check to this blaze of enthusiasm was that they made no mention of the name of Christ" (*Conf.*, 3.4). We need to keep in mind that although Augustine was now living in a pagan city, he still remembered his essentially Christian upbringing. Of course, we know that as a young man in Carthage he "used to go to sacrilegious shows and entertainments." He tells us so. "On the yearly festival of Berecynthia's Purification" he used to enjoy "the most degrading spectacles put on in honor of gods and goddesses" (*De Civitate Dei*, 2.4). Nevertheless, for Augustine from the very outset of his life, God was essentially the God made known to us in the person of Christ. So it is not surprising to find that he quickly turned from the pursuit of wisdom at the pen of Cicero to see how the God of the Bible made known in Jesus Christ should compare with the great works of his newfound hero.

"At Carthage," notes Henry Chadwick, "aged nineteen, he found that the seriousness of the questions raised by Cicero, especially about the quest for happiness moved him to pick up a Latin Bible" (*Augustine*, p. 11). "So I made up my mind to examine the holy Scriptures and see what kind of books they were," he tells us (*Conf.*, 3.5). The only Bible available in North Africa in Latin at the time was a book flawed by a bad translation and bad style. Furthermore, imagine Augustine's shock on reading such earthy stories as those of David and the accounts of all those bloody wars in the Old Testament after he had enjoyed the spiritual, high-sounding philosophy of Cicero in a text distinguished by its polished Latin style. "To me," he says, the Scriptures "seemed quite unworthy of comparison with the stately prose of Cicero" (*Conf.*, 3.5).

A "New" Religion from the East

CHRISTIANITY, and certainly the Christianity of the North African church (the sort that was available in the great basilica of St. Cyprian in Carthage just down the road, along the coast from the baths) was a very rigorous and unsophisticated expression of the faith. It still reflected memories of the persecutions of an earlier age, and in a rather authoritarian (almost Old Testament) way it demanded from its followers a morality and spirituality for which the young, sophisticated Augustine was certainly far from ready. However, as might well be expected, there was, especially in places like the university port town of Carthage, an alternative, "new" and "more spiritual" brand of ethereal religion. It appealed to the mind and the spiritual side of mankind. It had no place for all those crudities we find in the Old Testament stories. It would never lead a man or a woman to be embroiled with political, sociological, or moral issues of their day. It was above all that sort of thing. Christ was of course a central and important figure in this whole systematic view of the universe—but it was not the Christ of the cross or stable, enfleshed in history; rather, it was Christ as the principle of Wisdom reigning in the spiritual cosmos, accessible to all but only by the use of reason and intelligence. Such a religion promised to lead to true self-knowledge and enlightenment and liberate mankind (or at least the intelligentsia of Carthage if they would only listen) from all the shackles and encumbrances of a material world.

This religion had come from the East, of course. (It always does!) Its practitioners were to be known as the Manichees, and the philosophical message they brought was Manichaeism. The more we read about its teaching and its message, the more we can see that it was (and always will be) tailor-made for the Augustines of this world. It had two characteristics that were powerfully enticing to Augustine at this point in his pilgrimage. We need to note them very carefully, for they speak not only to Augustine and his age, to the climate of the declining years of the empire. It is also very apparent that such a philosophy speaks persistently throughout history, raising its false hopes in many times of decline and disintegration—not least in the climate of our own day.

In the first place, Manichaeism is dualistic; that is to say, it posits two kingdoms of equal power, eternal and totally separate at the heart of the universe—the kingdom of Light and the kingdom of Darkness. For Augustine, a search for an answer to the question of the origin of evil was to be a lifelong quest. Evil is real enough, but surely it cannot come from a good God. Like the man in the parable of the wheat and the tares, Augustine asks again and again throughout his pilgrimage—and with no little indignation—"Whence then, has it tares?"

The answer for the Manichee is simple, because in a sense he dispenses with the question. There are two kingdoms: one of good and one of evil. They are absolutely unconnected. So Manichaean philosophy encourages its disciples (all "Hearers," one of which Augustine soon keenly became) to love lofty things and to shun the things of the earth. Eventually such austerity will cause the lower nature of man to be "split off and shoved away from us, and, at the end of this existence, it will be defeated and wrapped up, all in a big, separate lump, as if in an eternal prison" (*De haeres*, 46.6). This schizoid solution to the problem sounded fine to the young Augustine. He even found himself singing about it from the Manichaean psalm book:

The vain garment of this flesh I put off, safe and pure; I caused the clean feet of my soul to trample confidently upon it.

By some kind of mutilation of the person, the Manichees maintain, at least part (the spiritual part) will remain unsoiled by the flesh or by matter. It will remain in a totally separate and separated area of one's life. Unfortunately, however, a view that divides the universe into two separate kingdoms also divides the person who perceives it in that way. The wise adviser, the husbandman in the parable of the wheat and the tares may well surprise us when he insists that "both should grow together." But clearly if we pull up the tares we shall pull up the wheat also. This Christian view of the universe and of personal wholeness is light-years away from the dualism propagated through Manichaeism.

In any event, we are compelled to admit that this dualistic philosophy was very convenient for the young, ambitious, lustful, guilt-ridden Augustine. Here was a view of life that seemed to solve the problem, to cut the Gordian knot. "I still thought that it is not we who sin but some other nature that sins within us. It flattered my pride to think that I incurred no guilt and, when I did wrong, not to confess it. . . . I preferred to excuse myself and blame this unknown thing which was in me but not part of me" (*Conf.*, 5.10). Yes, here indeed was the perfect schizoid prescription.

The second ingredient in Manichaeism, a sort of hardy annual throughout the whole of history, is its Gnostic element. Gnosticism—the belief that salvation comes through special knowledge—flatters

"I was led astray myself and led others astray in turn," writes Augustine of the period after his return to Thagaste from Carthage. *"We were alike deceivers and deceived in all our aims and ambitions, both publicly when we expounded our so-called liberal ideas, and in private through our service to what we called religion. In public we were cocksure, in private superstitious, and everywhere void and empty"* (Conf., *4.1*).

the intelligentsia and shuns everything in Christianity that might in any way bring the disciple into contact with the smell of the Sea of Galilee, the stench of the stable, or the simplicity of the worshiping shepherds. The Gnostic wants an elevated and elevating religion of the mind—a spiritual Jesus, untouched and unsoiled by history or the flesh. He prefers that redemption not involve the messy process of a human birth, the bloody mess of Calvary, or the stony reality of an empty tomb.

From the start, Gnosticism is far too spiritual for that kind of thing. And Manichaeism is strongly Gnostic in every way. It speaks of higher and lower eons and envisions a ladder of knowledge between the world of flesh and history and darkness on the one hand and the world of spiritual things, eternity, and light on the other. Again, such a view of the universe urges the disciple to flee from the flesh to the spirit, from the things of earth to the things of enlightened wisdom. Vegetarianism and various other special diets were (as they still are) all part of the package, part of the appeal of such a religion to a schizoid personality with a schizoid view of the universe.

Indeed, all the aspects of Manichaeism were like honey to the spiritually hungry young Augustine. It gave, after all, a neat and intellectually satisfying view of the universe. And it gave him the edge in any philosophical or religious argument during his days as a student at Carthage.

I always used to win more arguments than was good for me, debating with unskilled Christians who had tried to stand up for their faith in argument. With this quick succession of triumphs, the hot-headedness of a young man soon hardened into pig-headedness. As for this technique of argument, because I had set out on it after I had become a "Hearer" [among the Manichees], whatever I picked up by my own wits or by reading I willingly ascribed to the effects of their teaching. And so, from their preaching, I gained an enthusiasm for religious controversy, and from this I daily grew to love the Manichees

more and more. So it came about that, to a surprising extent, I came to approve of whatever they said—not because I knew any better, but because I wanted it to be true.

—De ii anim., 11

It is not surprising that Augustine should cling for a whole decade of his life there in Carthage and later in his teaching post in Rome to his association with the Manichees. At this stage in his journey they fitted his needs and aspirations very comfortably. Furthermore, they taught him a love for controversy—a love he never lost during his lifetime.

And so, complete with concubine and son Adeodatus, Augustine, a brilliant rhetorician, philosopher, and lawyer—and now as a keen Manichaean—returned A.D. 375 from his student days at Carthage back to Monica (now a widow) in Thagaste to teach his skills in his hometown. But, as we might expect, he did not go down very well at all. The return proved to be disastrous in every way.

CHAPTER THREE

A SHATTERED DREAM

A Strange Homecoming

WHAT a strange homecoming it must have been! The picture is almost absurd. For Augustine, just twenty-one years of age, brought home more luggage than he had left with, and most of it simply did not fit into Thagaste. After all, he was returning with a concubine, a small child, and above all his Manichaean superstitions. The fancy boy from Carthage was back in town and of course everybody knew all about him. The son of Monica and Patricius! The successful protégé of Romanianus, who readily shared his home and his family with Augustine and his retinue!

Monica was not at all pleased, nor did she make her son welcome. At first she would have none of it—neither the relationship with the concubine nor the strange new faith, which to her was little short of blasphemy. She refused to be under the same roof or sit at the same table with Augustine. Furthermore, she employed that most powerful weapon in battles of this kind—her tears. She shed more tears, Augustine tells us, for what she regarded as the "spiritual death" of her son than most mothers shed for "the bodily death of a son." Those tears, we are told, "streamed down and watered the earth in every place" when Monica "bowed her head in prayer" (*Conf.,* 3.11). And the prayer was always the same—"for Augustine, my son, my son." What a homecoming!

It is true that after a while Monica changed her mind and agreed to live with Augustine, his concubine, and Adeodatus and to "eat at the same table in" their home. Apparently, this change of mind came about through a dream.

"She dreamed that she was standing on a wooden rule, and coming towards her in a halo of splendour she saw a young man who smiled at her in joy, although she herself was sad and quite consumed with grief. He asked her the reason for her sorrow and her daily tears, not because he did not know, but because he had something to tell her. . . . When she replied that her tears were for the soul I had lost, he told her to take heart for, if she looked carefully, she would see that where she was, there also was I. And when she looked she saw me standing beside her on the same rule" (*Conf.,* 3.11).

Her hopes, her dreams, her prayers, and her tears—all were interwoven in a single fabric that spoke out one word and one word only—Augustine. After all, she had rehearsed all of this once before with her somewhat wayward husband, Patricius, and had brought him at the last, before his death, to faith. But now there was her son, and that was to prove a more difficult challenge.

Prayers like Monica's, salted with tears, are often answered. Both Monica and Augustine saw the dream as a kind of answer to her heartfelt prayers. In fact, the dream had as great an effect upon the son as upon the dreamer. Her prayers were answered again, she believed, "through the mouth of . . . a bishop who had lived his life in the Church and was well versed in the Scriptures" (*Conf.,* 3.12). Monica asked this bishop "as a favour" to have a word with her son, as he apparently often did with young pupils in need of spiritual guidance from a wise and holy father. However, the wise bishop refused to do this. Augustine reports that "he told her that I was still unripe for instruction, because . . . I was brimming over with the novelty of the heresy and had already upset a great many simple people" there in Thagaste with all the new ideas he brought back home from Carthage. The bishop knew what he was talking about, for he himself had been brought up as a Manichee and knew the pitfalls of such a heresy. "Leave him alone," the bishop counseled. "Just pray to God for him. From his own reading he will discover his mistakes and the debt of his profanity."

But apparently this advice did not sit well with Monica. She "persisted all the more with her tears and her entreaties," requesting that the good bishop should visit Augustine and discuss these matters with him. "At last he grew impatient and said 'Leave me and go in peace. It cannot be that the son of these tears should be lost.'" In later years, Monica used to say to Augustine "that she accepted these words as a message from heaven" (*Conf.*, 3.12). Once again, her prayers, she felt, were being answered.

The Influence of Friendship

Yet outwardly there was no change in the direction of her son's life and faith. He freely admits that during the years he spent between the age of nineteen and twenty-eight, "I was led astray myself and led others astray in turn. We were alike deceivers and deceived in all our different aims and ambitions, both publicly when we expounded our so-called liberal ideas, and in private through our service to what we called religion." It must have been quite the talk of the little town of Thagaste. "In public we were cocksure, in private superstitious and everywhere void and empty" (*Conf.*, 4.1).

Notice how suddenly Augustine begins to speak in the plural. It is here as it would always be in Augustine's life—"we." It is in fact impossible to understand Augustine fully in the singular. He did not like being alone. Later in life as a bishop, he would go to his study and write and read alone, but at all other times he was a man in community. Even here, at this early stage in Thagaste, we find him in the setting of a household with Monica (of course), his concubine, his son, and his newfound friends. Some of these friends were to stay with him and follow him in his journeyings—not only in his journeying around the Mediterranean world but also in those inner journeyings of faith and discipleship that led to his baptism as a Christian.

Augustine had a gift for friendship that later in his life, in the household of faith in which he lived as bishop in Hippo, blossomed into true community living and sharing. But even in these early years, we find him surrounded by companions and admirers. Listen to his eloquent tribute to those whom he counted as friends:

We could talk and laugh together and exchange small acts of kindness. We could join in the pleasure that books give. We could be grave or gay together. If we sometimes disagreed, it was without spite, as a man might differ with himself, and the rare occasions of dispute were the very spice to season our usual accord. Each of us had something to learn from others and something to teach in return. If any were away, we missed them with regret and gladly welcomed them when they came home. Such things as these are heartfelt tokens of affection between friends. They are signs to be read on the face and in the eyes, spoken by the tongue and displayed in countless acts of kindness. They can kindle a blaze to melt our hearts and weld them into one.

—Conf., *4.8*

What a rich and colorful testimony to the place of community and friendship in the spectrum of human relationships. Augustine had a genius for friendship and the gifts of an artist to commend it to us.

There was Alypius, who was "greatly attached to me because he thought I was a good and learned man, and I was fond of him because, although he was still young, it was quite clear that he had much natural disposition to goodness" (*Conf.*, 6.7). Alypius was from Thagaste, from one of the more influential families in the town. He had first been a pupil of Augustine when Augustine began to teach in Thagaste and then stayed with Augustine later in Carthage when Augustine returned there as professor. In fact, he was almost certainly the closest friend Augustine had and we shall keep bumping into him at every turning point in our story—in Carthage, in Rome, beside Augustine in the garden at his conversion, in Milan, and of course next to Augustine on that special night as he stood waiting to enter the waters of baptism in 387 at the hands of Ambrose, Bishop of Milan. He was to become especially close to Augustine in Rome, and in Augustine's own account in the *Confessions* he is not ashamed to spend several pages tracing the journey of their friendship and all that it was to mean in both of their lives. Alypius was eventually to become a bishop—Bishop of Thagaste—before Augustine.

Then, there was also Nebridius, "a young man of high principles and unexceptionable character." He was from a town near Carthage, and he became Augustine's traveling and intellectual companion in the years of pilgrimage and searching that led to his conversion and baptism. Like Augustine, Nebridius had been "caught in the pitfall of the most deadly error" (Manichaeism), but also like Augustine (and not a little, we can be sure, influenced by him) Nebridius was eventually to come to the bosom of the church.

Most certainly friendship was the dominant theme in Augustine's life, and he expresses it in ways and words that our contemporary world finds difficult to understand. "What," he writes later in life as a bishop living with friends in community, "should there be no bond of love between men? Truly there should be, so that no surer step towards God may be imagined than the love between man and man" (*On the Morals of the Catholic Church*, 1).

Death and Bereavement

In fact no biography of Augustine can avoid this theme. It was as though in this respect also he wanted the best of both worlds. We do not even know the name of the mother of his only son; she is dismissed from his life and his writings in a few sentences. He similarly speaks of the death of his father in only a passing sentence or two. Yet he devotes several pages of his autobiography to the death of his closest friend in these Thagaste days when he was a young man in his early twenties with a concubine and a son. Indeed, he laments and mourns here with an eloquence and a passion that is surpassed only when he is speaking and writing of Monica and her death: "During those years, when I first began to teach in Thagaste, my native town, I had found a very dear friend. We were both the same age, both together in the heyday of youth, and both absorbed in the same interests. We had grown up together as boys, gone to school together, and played together. . . . There was sweetness in our friendship, mellowed by the interests we shared" (*Conf.*, 4.4).

On his return to Thagaste, after his student days, Augustine took up this friendship again. Now, however, Augustine was that "cocksure" Manichaean "Hearer" and wanted to share with his friend back in his hometown his newfound faith and enthusiasm. Augustine tells us with the advantage of the hindsight of later years that as a boy the friend "had never held firmly or deeply to the true faith and I had drawn him away from it to believe in the same superstitious, soul-destroying fallacies which brought my mother to tears over me. Now, as a man, he was my companion in error and I was utterly lost without him."

It was then that the blow fell. Suddenly, after scarcely a year back together in Thagaste, Augustine writes,

My friend fell gravely ill of a fever. His senses were numbed as he lingered in the sweat of death, and when all hope of saving him was lost, he was baptized as he lay unconscious. I cared nothing for this, because I chose to believe that his soul would retain what it had learnt from me, no matter what was done to his body when it was deprived of sense. But no such a thing happened. New life came into him and he recovered. And as soon as I could talk to him—which was as soon as he could talk to me, for I never left his side since we were so dependent on each other—I tried to chaff him about his baptism, thinking that he too would make fun of it, since he had received it when he was quite incapable of thought and feeling. But by this time he had been told of it.

Conf., *4.4*

Augustine suffered one of the emotional earthquakes of his early life at this point. For his friend was far from ridiculing his baptism. In fact, he took it very seriously—so seriously that Augustine found himself looking at him from the opposite side of a great divide, the divide of living faith. His friend had in fact died in the sense that all those who are baptized die, passing through the waters of baptism to look at life from the other side, from a different point of view. So, Augustine records, "he looked at me in horror as though I were an enemy and in a strange, newfound attitude of self-reliance he warned me that if I wished to be his friend, I must never speak to him like that again." Something quite fundamental happened to Augustine at that point—a point that many biographers fail even to identify. "I was astonished and confused," he tells us. But there was worse to follow: "A few days after this, while I was away from him, the fever returned and he died" (*Conf.*, 4.4).

For the next five chapters of the *Confessions*, Augustine writes at length on the loss of his friend in particular and of the nature and power of friendship in general. In many ways this is the second milestone in Augustine's long journey and pilgrimage of conversion, which lasted from his nineteenth year until he was baptized at the age of thirty-three.

My heart grew sombre with grief, and wherever I looked I saw only death. My own country became a torment and my own home a grotesque abode of misery. All that we had done together was now a grim ordeal without him. My eyes searched everywhere for him, but he was not there to be seen. I hated all the places we had known together, because he was not in them and they could no longer whisper to me "Here he comes!" as they would have done had he been alive but absent for a while. . . . Tears alone were sweet to me, for in my heart's desire they had taken the place of my friend.

—*Conf., 4.4*

It was now Augustine's turn to weep. To the twentieth century, with its post-Freudian mindset, some of this seems very strange indeed and inevitably gives rise to questions about the nature of Augustine's sexuality. Yet two ingredients need to be affirmed at this point if we are to draw nearer to understanding our saint. The first is a point touched on already and is something to which we shall need to return again and again. Augustine was a man of passion—passion for men, for women, and ultimately for God. In many ways he was a David in the new Israel, and we know that David was capable of a love for Jonathan "surpassing the love of women." Furthermore, we may find that once again it is our contemporary outlook and fashion of mind that ought first to be questioned rather than the other way around. Earlier ages have frequently spoken of friendship with passion without necessarily insinuating perverted or unnatural relationships. It may be that it is our age that is imprisoned by Freudian categories and that earlier ages have enjoyed a freedom to embrace a wider spectrum of relationships with passion than our so-called liberated age seems able to do. Indeed, it may be that the lines of discipline that Augustine deliberately and specifically draws in the matter of friendships are precisely what gives him a freedom and true liberation in this area—a liberation our contemporary age craves but finds elusive.

"No friends are true friends unless you, my God, bind them fast to one another through that love which is sown in our hearts by the Holy Spirit, who is given to us" (*Conf.,* 4.4). In Christian theology, that is true of marriage as well as of friendship, and it certainly does not need to exclude passion. Strangely, it is the idolatry (often without passion) so evident in our Western society's view of matrimony that may be at the root of the wreckage so prevalent in twentieth-century married life. Perhaps Augustine has much to teach us in this area as in so many other areas.

Second, we shall never understand Augustine unless we see that from his earliest life, and certainly long before he wrote his famous *Rule of St. Augustine,* he was essentially a community man. In many ways he prepared the church for the Dark Ages by calling it to a lifestyle essentially oriented to community. St. Augustine would never have survived an antiseptic twentieth-century marriage with its two-point-five children. This would have been all too inhibiting, restrictive, and claustrophobic for him. He needed the warmth of an extended family in which close friendships are an essential building block. And so, here in Thagaste for that disastrous year, as afterward back in Carthage again, as during his Italian pilgrimage, and for nearly forty years as a bishop—always it is Augustine and his friends. "What is a man," he once exclaimed, "except his friends and his loves?"

Yet we must see this bereavement—the first to strike any real depths in him—as a blow that unsettled him considerably. The edifice of self-sufficiency was beginning to crumble and another turning point in the road to his ultimate conversion was reached. It was his lament for his dead friend after only one year back in Thagaste teaching rhetoric that ultimately convinced him that such a domestic arrangement was not going to work. "I left my native town. For my eyes were less tempted to look for my friend in a place where they had not grown used to seeing him. So from Thagaste I went to Carthage" (*Conf.*, 4.7).

Finally Fleeing the Nest

ONCE again Romanianus was supportive and helpfully directive to Augustine at this turning point in his life. Possibly Augustine shared with his patron many of his misgivings and frustrations with life in Thagaste. Certainly it had not worked out for all kinds of reasons, and so he sought out his benefactor for counsel. In later years, when writing to Romanianus, he was to remind him that

> *I disclosed to you alone among all my friends my hope and intention of returning to Carthage to seek a more brilliant career, although you hesitated somewhat on account of your innate love for your native city, because I was teaching there at the time, yet when you were unable to prevail upon the passionate desire of a youth who was stirring for what seemed better, you turned from the role of a dissuader to that of a helper by your extraordinary moderation and kindness. You provided me with everything necessary for my journey; you who had watched over my cradle, and, as it were, the nest of my studies, again in the same place supported my first attempts when I made bold to fly.*
>
> —Contra Academicos, *2.3*

And fly he did.

So A.D. 376 we follow him back again to Carthage, where he received, from the point of view of his career, an advantageous post as professor of rhetoric. Certainly, from every point of view, there was no way that he could have remained in Thagaste. At twenty-two he needed (for the sake of his career as much as for anything else) to flee the nest for the richer environment and more influential contacts that only the city of Carthage (itself second only to Rome) would afford him. In his new position, Augustine would meet all kinds of people who in their turn had contacts in the court at Rome and Milan at the heart of the empire.

For too long the court at Rome had been in the grip of the military, who had little time or inclination for the arts, philosophy, or men of letters. Emperors such as Valentinian I had little place in their lives for subtlety of language and styles of rhetoric. However, as is so often the case, a self-made, aggressive father covets for his son those very qualities and talents he himself lacks. So with Valentinian and his son. There was an assured place at court therefore for the elderly and famous professor of rhetoric Ausonius, who was virtually pulled out of retirement to be the tutor to the emperor's son. On the death of Valentinian I in the autumn of the year before Augustine took up his new post in Carthage, Ausonius found himself in that potentially most influential of roles—the favorite of the new young occupant of the throne. Ausonius had real power as the figurehead of a new emerging aristocracy of lettered men in the empire, and it so happened that both his son and son-in-law arrived in Carthage as proconsuls at the very time Augustine returned there as professor of rhetoric—a significantly prominent position in the literary society of that great city.

Symmachus, a Roman senator, man of letters, and cousin of Ambrose, who helped secure Augustine's apointment as professor of literature and rhetoric in the imperial city of Milan

Ambition and Success

THEN, of course, there was Symmachus, an influential senator in Rome who also had links with Carthage. He had formerly come to Carthage as proconsul in 371 and now retained in Carthage a large villa. Symmachus was a man of letters converted to Wisdom and typical of that whole race of figures who emerged in the Roman Empire in the age of Late Antiquity. He sought a cultured maturity in old age, living in quiet and untroubled surroundings, free from worldly and political concerns, and free to read and reflect upon the literary masters of the age. Furthermore, it happens that this same Symmachus was cousin to Ambrose, who had only recently been consecrated as Bishop of Milan by popular appeal on December 7, 374, and was now sitting in Milan at the helm of political as well as ecclesiastical influence.

There was a kind of network stretching across the Mediterranean to Milan in the north, Carthage in the south, and Rome (of course) at the center of it all. On his return to Carthage, Augustine had access to this network, and there is some evidence that once he left behind Thagaste, it was the challenge of his new post and the stimulation afforded by his new friends and contacts, together

with ambition and success in his career, that temporarily suppressed and sublimated the deeper yearnings and aspirations of his soul. After all, he had done well. There was no reason now why he should not do even better.

In any case, it was not long before Augustine was making a name for himself. He won a prize for a set poem and was crowned as a kind of poet laureate by the proconsul, Vindicianus. In fact, he soon became a friend of Vindicianus. He was "a man of deep understanding, who had an excellent reputation for his great skill as a doctor" (*Conf.*, 4.3). Augustine does not tell us, but we know from other sources that this good doctor had formerly enjoyed a great reputation at court for curing indigestion—a claim to fame indeed in an empire that frequently overindulged in rank gluttony.

This father figure (perhaps a prototype of Ambrose in later years) won the admiration and attention of the young Augustine, who "listened intently and without fail to what he had to say, for though he was not a gifted speaker, his lively mind gave weight and charm to his words." Augustine notes that "in the course of our conversation, he learned that I was an enthusiast for books of astrology and in a kind and fatherly way he advised me to throw them away and waste no further pains upon such rubbish because there were other more valuable things to be done" (*Conf.*, 4.3). And, indeed, there were, although Augustine stubbornly remained unconvinced and kept the books.

By this time Augustine was operating, as he tells us, "a word shop" in Carthage. Surely now was the the time for him to write his first book. He wanted very much to make his name as an author of distinction in the literary circle at Carthage.

The First Book

HAPPILY, history has spared us the opportunity to assess Augustine's first endeavor as a young, somewhat self-conscious author. He tells us that by "some chance the book was lost" and neither he nor history possesses a copy. In "two or three volumes" our young ambitious aesthete wrote a work entitled *Beauty and Proportion,* dedicating it to "Hierius, the great public speaker in Rome." He had never seen Hierius, "but I admired his brilliant reputation for learning and had been greatly struck by what I had heard of his speeches" (*Conf.,* 4.14)—though he was able to admit that he had been even more "impressed by the admiration which other people had for him."

Here was flagrant ambition, and Augustine is not ashamed to admit to it in his searching spiritual journal when he recalls with some embarrassment as an older man the overriding motivations at this point in his life. "In my pride I was running adrift at the mercy of every wind. . . . Yet I found pleasure in giving my mind to the problem of beauty and proportion, the work which I dedicated to him. Although I found no others to admire it, I was proud of it myself" (*Conf.,* 4.14). He was "about twenty-six or twenty-seven years old" when he wrote *Beauty and Proportion.* Yet for many years—in fact, ever since he had first become a Manichee—there had been another contact he had wanted to make—a Manichaean bishop by the name of Faustus. He was so highly respected among the Manichees that Augustine was determined to meet him and put before him some of the questions that were increasingly disturbing his mind.

Augustine had already "read a great many scientific books" about "the created world, about mathematics and the visible evidence of the stars." But when he compared these sciences of his day "with the teaching of Manes, who had written a great deal on these subjects," it all seemed "extremely incoherent." There were the other misgivings he wished to share with Faustus, since "other members of the sect whom I happened to meet were unable to answer the questions" that he could no longer silence in his own mind. He had been assured by these other members of the sect that once Faustus had arrived, "he would have no difficulty in giving me a clear explanation of my queries and any other more difficult problems which I might put forward. Augustine "awaited the coming of this man Faustus with the keenest expectation. . . . At last he arrived."

Disillusionment and Unrest

AUGUSTINE found Faustus to be "a man of agreeable personality with a pleasant manner of speech, who pattered off the usual Manichean arguments with a great deal more than the usual charm" (*Conf.,* 5.6). He was a fine, eloquent, polished speaker, and the "ease with which he found the right words to clothe his thoughts" did not go unnoticed or indeed unappreciated by the young professor of rhetoric. However, the searching mind of Augustine refused to be fobbed off with fine words. He tells us that he "did not care what words [Faustus] used to garnish the dish." Perhaps it takes one rhetorician to uncover the traps and allurements in the words another tunefully employs!

Faustus, like Augustine, knew what rhetoricians have always known—how "to acquire that eloquence that is essential to persuade men of your case, to unroll your opinions before them." But this time, for Augustine, opinions and eloquence were not enough. Now there was a new and telling urgency to the debate. Augustine did not want more opinions. Now it was a question of matters of fact and truth. He had already learned "that a statement is not necessarily true because it is wrapped in fine language or false because it is awkwardly expressed." In spite of what he might have written in his book *Beauty and Proportion,* aesthetics were not the final arbiters of truth. Faustus "had read some of Cicero's speeches, one or two books of Seneca, some poetry, and such books as had been written in good Latin by members of his sect," but it was not merely spiritual, philosophical, or aesthetic matters but rather questions concerning scientific truth about the material and created universe that were now uppermost in Augustine's mind.

There were clearly difficulties in the early stages of the relationship between Augustine and Faustus, and yet they eventually became good friends and had extended discussions together, enjoying the "friendly give-and-take of conversation." But the "enthusiasm for literature" that often brought them together was not in itself enough to satisfy the eager, questing mind of Augustine. For his part, Faustus was "not entirely unaware of his limitations" (*Conf.,* 5.7), yet he was obviously unable to resolve the many problems that troubled Augustine.

And notice the shift of emphasis in these problems. Augustine's quest remained the same— "Truth. How the very marrow of my soul within me yearned for it!"—but he no longer sought merely the truth of philosophy or even of the "higher things alone" as was the case when he first read Cicero way back in his student days and during his first days in Carthage. Now he sought also the truth of science. Astrology had given way to astronomy. Mathematics, "the succession of the seasons," and "the visible evidence of the stars"—such truths must belong to the whole truth and be seen as one. It was to be an embarrassment later in life whenever he heard a Christian talk in such a way as to show his ignorance of scientific matters. Augustine concedes that such errors can be forgiven, that they are more or less harmless if the mistaken person "does not know the true facts about material things" and also providing that "he holds no beliefs unworthy" or contrary to true beliefs about God. But it was beginning to dawn on Augustine that the claims of Manes, who "dared to pose as teacher, sole authority, guide, and leader of all whom he could convince of his theories" could be shown to be erroneous by the counterclaims of science. And so, with a passion so typical of Augustine, he began to denounce as repugnant the claims he had formerly championed, to urge that they "should be entirely rejected" (*Conf.,* 5.5).

This realization, linked with his disillusionment about Faustus, brought him at the age of twenty-nine in the year 383 to the point where he abandoned "all my endeavours to make progress in the sect. . . . I did not cut myself off entirely from the Manichees, but . . . decided to be content with them for the time being, unless something preferable clearly presented itself to me." At last he felt he was released "from the trap in which I had been caught."

A stained glass window in the basilica in Hippo depicting Augustine's duplicitous farewell to Monica as he left Carthage for Rome. "I deceived her with the excuse that I had a friend whom I did not want to leave until the wind rose and his ship could sail. It was a lie, told to my own mother—and to such a mother, too!" (Conf., 5.8).

On the Move Again

AND all the while Monica was pouring "out her tears" and offering "her heart-blood in sacrifice" for her son. The foundations of his life had been shaken by the death of his friend, and now the foundations were shifting once again. In every way Augustine was on the move. In fact he was literally taking to the road again and relocating his life.

He was disillusioned with Carthage. For one thing the students in Carthage were "beyond control"; their behavior was "disgraceful." They would "come blustering into the lecture-rooms like a troop of maniacs and upset the orderly arrangements which the master [had] made in the interests of his pupils" (*Conf., 5.8*). Their recklessness was unbelievable. As a student, he writes, "I had refused to take part in this behaviour, but as a teacher I was obliged to endure it in others."

When the opportunity came, he decided to leave for Rome, where connections in the international network of the literary underworld promised him "better earnings" and stronger enticements. Alypius had already left to study law in Rome, where "he became obsessed with extraordinary cravings for gladiatorial shows." So to Rome Augustine would go and join his friend.

But what about Monica? She must somehow or other be left behind. Augustine needed to break loose again. His restless heart had not yet found its home. "She wept bitterly to see me go and followed me to the water's edge, clinging to me with all her strength in the hope that I would either come home or take her with me. I deceived her with the excuse that I had a friend whom I did not want to leave until the wind rose and his ship could sail. It was a lie, told to my own mother—and to such a mother, too!" (*Conf., 5.8*).

But Monica was not deceived. Her love and intuition told her what she could scarcely bare to know. So, "she would not go home without me and it was all I could do," he recalls, "to persuade her to stay that night in a shrine dedicated to St. Cyprian, not far from the ship. During the night, secretly, I sailed away, leaving her alone to her tears and her prayers. . . . The wind blew and filled our sails, and the shore disappeared from sight."

Monica "went back to her home," and Augustine, her restless son, "went on to Rome," the capital of the empire.

CHAPTER FOUR

ILLUSIONS OF SUCCESS—
BREAKDOWN AND
BREAKTHROUGH

Life in Rome

AUGUSTINE had not been happy at Carthage and he was not to be happy in Rome. "As for myself, life at Carthage was a real misery and I loathed it: but the happiness I hoped to find at Rome was not real happiness" (*Conf.,* 5.8). The journey from Carthage to Ostia (the port of Rome) was not particularly difficult. (As the crow flies, it was only 350 miles or so: just over two days' sailing time.) The traffic between Carthage and Ostia was well serviced by several ships each week, and contact with the heart of the empire was not difficult. Yet strangely, all his life, Augustine disliked travel of any kind intensely; as Frederick van der Meer notes, "like Erasmus he could bear neither the sea nor the winter cold" (*Augustine the Bishop,* p. 236).

After such a tedious and difficult cutting of the cord with Monica, we might well suppose that Augustine would dock in Ostia with heavy foreboding. His departure from Carthage had at best been hasty and at worst rather clumsy and erratic. For example, in addition to deceiving his mother, he had also failed to inform Romanianus of his intentions to leave—Romanianus, a consistent and caring benefactor who from the first had made possible Augustine's education and who, by Augustine's own admission, had watched over the "nest of his studies." He had advised and helped Augustine in the past at important turning points in his life. Indeed, he owed his very presence in Carthage both for the first and second time to the generous support and helpful guidance afforded to him by Romanianus. And now without a word,

while Romanianus was away (doubtless on yet another of his many missions overseas), Augustine set sail for his new life in Rome. He had not made a very good job at all of this bridge passage in the symphony of his life and doubtless the scenes of a distracted Monica and a disenchanted Romanianus were haunting him as the ship approached the huge port of Ostia, bringing him to the ancient city of Rome.

At first, he must have felt very much an alien, strangely irrelevant in the sheer size and extent of Rome—the center and mecca of its empire. After all, everything from his features and the color of his skin to his accent and pronunciation of Latin would have made it obvious that he came from overseas. As Peter Brown so tellingly says, in Rome and Italy "he would have been like a Westernized Russian in the nineteenth century, established in Paris" (*Augustine of Hippo,* p. 33).

In the time of Augustine, Rome boasted one and a quarter million inhabitants—a large population indeed in the ancient world. It had about it something of a fading nostalgia, almost the sacrament of a glory that had long departed. Indeed, if the glory of Rome lay in its imperial court, then the glory had literally departed: it had gone north to Milan. Of course, the outward, visible, and tangible signs of its glory and its history remained intact—at least until A.D. 410, when the city was overrun for the first of several times by hordes of Goths and barbarians. There was still much, of course, of the huge and impressive forum with its columns, its magnificent proud statues, steps of marble leading up to grand and spacious courtyards, and, it is recorded, something like three thousand palaces—the houses of the rich plutocrats who still inhabited or at least had a base in the capital city of the empire.

But signs of poverty and squalor lay in hard and contradictory juxtaposition to those evidences of wealth. It was a city of the rich but also a city of slaves and plebians. It has been the fate of large cosmopolitan cities throughout history to collect (generally in a small areas frequently bounded or determined by rivers and seas) violence and culture, abject poverty and decadent wealth, all thrust cheek and jowl together in the spaciousness of anonymity and at the same time the confusion and anger associated perhaps at its most vicious with a colony of rats. Rome was a home to crime and violence at the games as well as to colonies of literary and artistically sophisticated disciples of every cult, school, and philosophy that the ancient world at large could invent.

It was to such a milieu, to such an explosive environment, that the young Augustine (he was not yet thirty years old) had fled. He did what we all would do in such a situation. Occupants of over-large cities plant their roots in ghettos. The only possible counterbalance to sprawling anonymity is a network of ghettos that transcend the cultures and languages of the larger world. Augustine was still, after all, a "Hearer" in the sect of the Manichees, and so he sought out the contacts that were open to him there. He took lodgings with a Manichee who was also a "Hearer" in a ghetto where aliens from the Levantine countries, Egypt, and the Orient banded together near the great warehouses on the very banks of the river Tiber.

Problems and Disappointments in Rome

AUGUSTINE was to spend just over a year in the eternal city—a rather miserable year. It is hard at this distance for us to see quite why he should have chosen to flee from Africa to Italy. Even in later years, reflecting on this chapter of his life, Augustine found it difficult to sort out the motives for this apparently sudden and swiftly conceived plan. "It was not because I could earn higher fees and greater honours" he tells us, though he is not ashamed to confess that such rewards were "promised me by my friends, who urged me to go" (*Conf.*, 5.8), and "naturally these considerations influenced" him. It's almost as though he too had fallen prey to the fantasy common throughout history that the streets of large cities are paved with gold.

In summarizing his own motivations, Augustine tells us that "the most important reason and almost the only one" for which he made this journey was that he had been led to suppose that "the behaviour of young students at Rome was quieter." Apparently "discipline was stricter and they were not permitted to rush insolently and just as they pleased into the lecture-rooms of teachers who were not their own masters. In fact they were not admitted at all without the master's permission" (*Conf.*, 5.8). At least that was in sharp contrast with the behavior of his rowdy and ill-disciplined students at Carthage.

At first he began to teach in his house, where he collected a number of pupils who had heard of his reputation, and through them and all his contacts, his reputation began to grow. What he had not been told, however, was that although students in Rome were not given to rioting or the more straightforward forms of hooliganism he experienced in Carthage, "they were quite unscrupulous, and justice meant nothing to them compared with the love of money" (*Conf.*, 5.12). Specifically, he was to learn to his cost that they "would plot together to avoid paying their master his fees and would transfer in a body to another."

Therefore, although it was not quite a case of out of the frying pan of Carthage into the fire of Rome, it is nevertheless true that the happiness he had hoped to find in Rome eluded him in almost every way from the very outset. He got off to a bad start: "at Rome, I was at once struck down by illness" (*Conf.*, 5.9). It was serious and almost carried him off—doubtless a fever and infection not totally unrelated to the pollution and environment of the capital city, which overlooked the river. His fever rose, and he tells us, with the benefit of hindsight, that he "came close to dying." Happily, he was in the house of a Manichee, and he was cared for by his host during both his illness and convalescence. However, he attributes his recovery not to his Manichaean friends but directly and unapologetically to the constant prayers of Monica, who, though knowing apparently nothing of his predicament and malady, nevertheless, "never let a day go by . . . each morning and night" as she went to church to plead "that the soul of her son might be saved." And, "so it was that [God] healed my sickness" (*Conf.*, 5.9-10).

Friendships and Connections in Rome

THERE was at least one piece of good news among all the unpleasantness Augustine experienced during his brief stay in Rome: Alypius. "I found him in Rome when I arrived. He became very closely attached to me" (*Conf.*, 6.10). Alypius was from Thagaste, and "his people were one of the leading families." He was younger than Augustine, having been one of his students when he first began to teach both in Thagaste and later on in Carthage. Rather against his own wishes, and more from the prompting of his parents, Alypius was pursuing his legal studies and had gone ahead to Rome, taking the post of chancellor to the Italian treasury. There his lifelong friendship with Augustine ripened and deepened.

Throughout the whole story of Augustine we are never very far from his friends, his mother, or his hero figures. Although Alypius was younger than Augustine, he was nevertheless something of a hero figure to the older man from the outset. He had what Augustine chose to call a "natural disposition to goodness." In a word he was a man of high principles, earnestly seeking the truth and wide open to the influence of his older friend and teacher.

Although Augustine goes to some lengths in his *Confessions* to assure us of the influence, goodness, and integrity of Alypius, he also relates a story that is meant to stress a point he taught for the rest of his life after his conversion—namely, that goodness and integrity are not enough. In our contemporary world we are shocked by the bloodthirsty violence that frequently erupts among civilized and well-trained people once they are in a large crowd stimulated and teased by games and sports. And yet we should not be surprised by this phenomenon. It is as ancient as the ancient world itself. Alypius had always been opposed to any attendance at such events, not least in Rome, where there was crowd participation in events on a huge scale and where the springs of human violence

When Alypius attended the gladiatorial shows, his disapproval dissolved. "He revelled in the wickedness of the fighting and was drunk with the fascination of bloodshed," Augustine reports. "He was no longer the man who had come to the arena but simply one of the crowd" (Conf., 6.8). Painting by Jean Leon Gerome

were constantly released. As one writer so eloquently and sensitively puts it, "the love of contest and the lust of blood,

> *Dwell in the depths of man's original heart,*
> *And at mere shows and games of wise and good*
> *Will not from their barbaric homes depart,*
> *But half-asleep await their time, and then*
> *Bound forth like tigers from their jungle den.*

At that time in Rome, as now at games and shows in the big cities of our world many centuries later,

> *All the curious wickerwork of thought,*
> *Of logical result and learned skill,*
> *Of precepts with examples interwrought,*
> *Of high ideals and determinate will,*
> *The careful fabric of ten thousand hours*

> *Is crushed beneath the moment's brutal powers.*
> —Lord Houghton, "The Fall of Alypius"

"High ideals and determinate will" proved not to be enough to restrain even Alypius once he was exposed, apparently against his will, to the lust and cruelty of the gladiatorial games of Rome. The roar of the crowd enticed him, and he found himself obsessed by the savage passions released in him.

Augustine had always counseled against attending these events and continued to do so all his life. Such admonitions arise not from a heart that is seeking to be indifferent to human passion but rather from experience that knows all too well the untamed, destructive powers latent within everyone, powers that need direction, not exploitation. When Alypius saw the blood spilled in the gladiatorial show, reports Augustine, "it was as though he had drunk a deep draft of savage passion. Instead of turning away, he fixed his eyes upon the scene and drank in all its frenzy, unaware of what he was doing. He revelled in the wickedness of the fighting and was drunk with the fascination of bloodshed. He was no longer the man who had come to the arena, but simply one of the crowd" (*Conf.,* 6.8). Such a description could come straight out of the newspapers of our own age, describing the apparently inexplicable eruptions of crowd violence in stadiums in many parts of our world today. It could be said of Augustine that "he knew what was in man." This is not to say that his last word on mankind is pessimistic but only that his first word on the human condition is realistic—and indeed, it is only when this is the case that the last word can be truly optimistic. Those who write off Augustine have often not really wrestled with or truly become aware of the incredible potential for self-destruction in the human race.

But back to Rome, Alypius, and Augustine. Aliens they were in an alien land, yet it was not long before Augustine made his way into an international community of literary boffins and Manichaean friends. By this time Augustine was rapidly losing sympathy with the philosophy and teaching of the Manichees, but an issue arose that served to forge a bond among all those from the ghetto of which he was now a conspicuous member—an increasingly intolerant and powerful Christian church. Although, in his religion and philosophy, Augustine's mind was once again on the move, he was able to use recommendations and support from his Manichaean friends to bend the ear of Symmachus, prefect of the city of Rome, to secure his appointment as professor of literature and rhetoric in the imperial city of Milan.

Symmachus was himself an alien from the provinces of the empire, conservative in outlook and still wishing to support the old pagan slogans and trophies in the face of a disintegrating empire and an increasingly aggressive institutional Christianity. In the spring of 384 Symmachus had actively taken steps to persuade the emperor to reestablish the traditional pagan religious celebrations in Rome. Only a few years earlier, public funds had been withdrawn from all the public pagan ceremonies. This move would be politically analagous to a government today declaring that certain Christian festivals were no longer to be regarded as public holidays and that other days (of a different political coloring) would be deemed public festivals in their place.

Promotion in Rome

To Symmachus and his friends from the *ancien regime,* such an action on the part of the state represented increasing power on the part of the church. Symmachus made an appeal for toleration. The wording is as old as the hills and frequently recurs at such moments of religious and political realignment: "Not by one way alone can man attain to so great a mystery." However, Symmachus had not allowed for the contrary powers of persuasion from his relative Bishop Ambrose of Milan. Situated next to the seat of power—the imperial court and the boy emperor Valentinian II in the northern capital—Ambrose was swift to remind the young emperor that as a catechumen in the church of Jesus Christ, he could allow no place for national deities in his policies.

So Symmachus and those he represented were defeated. Yet what if he could make sure that the new minister of propaganda in Milan was anti-Christian? That would be a subtle blow to deal the bishop. It was, in fact, in his power to nominate such an individual, and beyond this Symmachus still wielded considerable power through his writings as a man of culture, influence, and insight in the Roman world of his day.

In any case, by the autumn of 384 this much was clear: Augustine was disenchanted both with Rome and Manichaeism, and he was ready to move. "So when the Prefect of Rome [Symmachus] received a request from Milan to find a teacher of literature and elocution for the city, with the promise that travelling expenses would be charged to public funds, I applied for the appointment, armed with recommendations from my friends who were so fuddled with the Manichean rigamarole. This journey was to mean the end of my association with them, though none of us knew it at the time. Eventually Symmachus, who was then Prefect, set me a test to satisfy himself of my abilities and sent me to Milan" (*Conf.,* 5.13).

Our perspective on this event permits us to appreciate its irony. In making this appointment, Symmachus was bringing together two men, Ambrose and Augustine, who more than any other two would champion politically and theologically the very orthodox Christianity that Symmachus most abhorred, the very church that was dealing the final blows to the already crumbling and disintegrating superstructure of the empire.

Of course, from the point of view of his profession, Augustine had done very well indeed by this move. He was to be transported to Milan without expense in public vehicles and to receive a fixed salary in addition to his fees. It was Symmachus himself who had once noted that "The high road to office is often laid open by literary success." Why should this not be so for the young professor Augustine? As he traveled at the government's expense to the imperial city of Milan, he could be forgiven for reflecting on the success of another African of his age, Aurelius Victor, who said of himself, "I grew up in the country, the son of a poor uneducated father: in my time, I have come, through my pursuit of literature, to live the life of a nobleman" (*De Caesaribus,* 20.5).

Yet in reality that was not how it felt to Augustine as he arrived in Milan. He tells us in his *Confessions* that his real quest and journey was Godward: "I was looking for you outside myself and I did not find the God of my own heart. I had reached the depths of the ocean. I had lost all faith and was in despair of finding the truth" (*Conf.,* 6.1). Hardly the cry of a man scaling the heights of a new pinnacle in his career.

Milan: The Court and the Bishop

As it turned out, Augustine's was not to be the success story that it might have appeared to be. Milan and the presence of the emperor and the court there might have seemed to be the gateway to the empire, to high position, and to success. But actually, it was to turn out to be the place of another presence and the gateway to another, very different kingdom.

The developing drama had two ingredients that bring us to the crisis of our story. The first ingredient—friends and acquaintances—sets the stage, and indeed each will have their part to play. But the second ingredient—the story of another journey and another pilgrimage, of which the long journey from Rome to Milan is but an outward sign—is more important.

Augustine journeyed inwardly a good deal further than ever he could outwardly, even if he had had the whole landscape of this planet to roam through. We shall see him as his friends saw him, struggling on the longest journey in the world— the journey from head to heart and from heart to will. We shall watch the pressures mounting, bringing Augustine to that point of breakdown, to that most blessed of moments for anyone, when breakdown becomes breakthrough and when the crisis is resolved not so much by surrender as by transcendence.

But first we need to set the stage. Even if the characters on this particular stage are only secondary in importance for this drama, they are nevertheless crucial. Indeed, it was increasingly the case for Augustine that life was to be lived in a community of friends. There is strong evidence that he never liked to be alone for very long; he might have been a prima donna but never a soloist. Later in life, as a bishop, apart from the long periods he spent in study, writing, and reading, he was always with friends in community. Indeed, the seeds of his later formal community life are there at the outset in his early life and become clearly evident on his arrival in Milan.

And we might guess that it was not long before Monica was on the scene again, arriving in Milan ostensibly to deal with property inherited from Patricius, her late husband. How very convenient! But she had brought quite an entourage with her also to be part of the new professor's household. There was her elder son Navigius and two nephews, Rusticus and Lastidianus. After a rough crossing from North Africa, during which

the ship had been in some considerable danger, Monica, who had faced "all perils with sure faith," was once again at her son's side.

Augustine was able to greet her with some good news: he was not a "Christian, but at least [he] was no longer a Manichee" (*Conf.*, 6.1). He admits that by this time, at the age of thirty, "I had been rescued from falsehood, even if I had not yet grasped the truth." Monica was more convinced than ever that before she left this life, she would see him a faithful Christian. All this gave added zest to her longings and prayers and her daily visits to the local cathedral and to the shrines of the saints.

Also present in Milan in the newly established household of professor Augustine was his concubine and their little son, Adeodatus, now just twelve years old. That arrangement, however, was not to last for very long. Augustine's presence was required at court from time to time to deliver tedious panegyrics and eulogies in the name of the state and its young boy emperor, and he had to establish himself in a level of society appropriate to his position and his career. To that end he would need a legal wife.

"I was being urged incessantly to marry," he tells us in rather petulant tones. "My mother had done all she could to help, for it was her hope that, once I was married, I should be washed clean of my sins by the saving waters of baptism" (*Conf.*, 6.13). Indeed, he had already made a proposal and been accepted, though the marriage was necessarily going to be delayed by the fact that the young girl concerned was only twelve years old, almost two years under nubile age. Planning for the marriage progressed nonetheless, and key to it all was Augustine's separation from the woman who had been faithful to him for many years and who had mothered his son. "She went back to Africa," he tells us with some shame, "vowing never to give herself to any other man, and left with me the son whom she had borne me" (*Conf.*, 6.15). Far from solving problems, however, this seemed only to compound them. Augustine was "impatient at the delay of two years which had to pass before" his prospective bride could marry him. So, he tells us quite blatantly, he took another mistress. Add to this the bereavement he truthfully and honorably confesses at the loss of his concubine and we can begin to see something of the early ingredients of an emotional breakdown.

Happily, Alypius, who had become "very closely attached" to Augustine in Rome, went with him to Milan so that they could be together "and also because he wanted to put his legal studies into practice" (*Conf.*, 6.10). Nebridius was also in Milan now. "He had left his own town near Carthage and Carthage itself, where he had spent much of his time. He had given up his house and his family's rich estate in the country and had left his mother, who had refused to come with him" (*Conf.*, 6.10). (One thing is certain—there would not have been room for two Monicas in Milan and certainly not under the same roof!) But Augustine frankly also tells us that Nebridius "had come to Milan for no other purpose than to live with me, so that we might be together in our fervent search for truth and wisdom" (*Conf.*, 6.10). And so Milan was the point of convergence in their friendships.

"We were," says Augustine, "like three hungry mouths" waiting for God to grant them the nourishment of his truth and his love. What a party there must have been at the young professor's home: a strange little colony from North Africa living together with Monica presiding! Already,

even at this stage of questing and instability, Augustine was intuitively seeking the life of community. What in these early days was only a dream would in later years become the chief cornerstone of his pastoral strategy as a bishop.

Augustine tells us that in those turbulent Milan days, a group of his friends (primarily Alypius and Nebridius)

who detested the bustle and worry of life had all but decided to live a life of peace away from the crowd. We had thought over this project and discussed it together a great deal. The plan was to arrange this life of leisure by pooling our possessions and using such money as we had between us to create a common fund. In the spirit of sincere friendship none of us would claim this or that as his own, but all would be thrown together and the whole would belong to each and to all. We thought that there might be about ten members of our community. Some of them were very wealthy, especially Romanianus, who came from my own town. He had been one of my closest friends since boyhood and had come to Milan on some urgent legal business connected with his affairs. He was most enthusiastic about our project, and as he was far richer than the rest of us, his opinions carried great weight.

—Conf., *6.14*

It was clearly an important idea and theme for Augustine, a foreshadowing of what was later to be realized in his community life as a bishop in Hippo for nearly forty years and what was to be the basis of his famous rule of St. Augustine with its guidelines and insights into community life.

The Influence of Ambrose

BUT the stage is not yet quite complete—for the principal and most active character in this drama was to be a man small in stature but great in influence—Ambrose, Bishop of Milan. Upon his arrival in Milan, Augustine tells us, "I found your devoted servant the bishop Ambrose, who was known throughout the world as a man whom there were few to equal in goodness. . . . This man of God received me like a father and, as bishop, told me how glad he was that I had come. My heart warmed to him, not at first as a teacher of the truth, which I had quite despaired of finding in your church, but simply as a man who showed me kindness. I listened attentively when he preached to the people" (*Conf.*, 5.13).

That is an understatement. Augustine was fascinated by St. Ambrose, who was to become the most formative of all his father and hero figures and on whose model of the episcopate Augustine was later to pattern his own life and ministry. The bishop was fourteen years older than Augustine, and prior to Augustine's arrival in Milan he had served as bishop for nearly eleven years. Everything about this noble patrician spoke with authority.

It is hard to overestimate the influence one man can have upon the history of the whole world. If he is formative in the life of an even greater man who in his turn will influence a great many people, then the extent of that influence is almost beyond calculation. If in the history of the church Ambrose slew his thousands, then in his turn St. Augustine has slain his ten thousands.

In the first place, Augustine found in Ambrose a rhetorician whose eloquence he greatly admired.

Ambrose was a formidable expository preacher and teacher of the Christian faith. He was also a writer, an administrator, and an astute politician. In the political intrigues of the Arian party at the court in Milan, it was Ambrose who had withstood even to her face the mother of the young boy emperor. Justina was a woman of power and ruthlessness but she found her match in little Ambrose when she ordered the troops of the imperial to lay seige to the basilica in which she had imprisoned him along with his congregation.

At last, here was the sort of hero that Augustine had spent much of his life seeking. Here was a model and a powerful advocate of the truth of orthodox Christianity. Augustine could not stay away from the new and immensely impressive basilica in which Ambrose could be heard almost daily expounding the Scriptures. "Every Sunday I listened as he preached the word of truth to the people" (*Conf.*, 6.3).

As it turned out, the way in which Ambrose expounded the Scriptures had a special significance for Augustine, who by this stage was increasingly disillusioned with Manichaeism. He tells us that it was Ambrose who showed him at last "how to interpret the ancient Scriptures of the law and the prophets in a different light from that which had previously made them seem absurd" (*Conf.*, 6.4). In a word, Ambrose illuminated the meaning of Scripture by expounding its spiritual and allegorical significance, releasing it from a kind of fourth-century fundamentalism and making it the source of powerful and prayerful illumination in the Spirit.

Although Ambrose was particularly successful in dealing with Scripture in a way that was new to Augustine, he also managed to impart in general a whole new insight into the Christian faith—an insight that was profound and free from so many of the perversions and absurdities Augustine had formerly regarded as an inevitable part of the incredible Christian creeds. "I had been howling my complaints not against the Catholic faith but against something quite imaginary which I had thought up in my own head" (*Conf.,* 6.3). At last, whether Augustine knew it or not, he was receiving first-hand and first-class instruction in the Christian religion. In effect, Ambrose was doing the job which had to be done if ever Augustine with his keen mind was to become a baptized and practicing Christian.

This is not to suggest that information can ever be a substitute for faith. Rather the point is that faith must not be built upon ignorance: it requires first the facts, which in their turn can make ultimate sense only in the light of faith. Augustine admits that he still waited to be "just as certain of these things which were hidden from my sight as that seven and three make ten" (*Conf.,* 6.4). But he was slowly beginning to see that most of our life is built not upon that kind of mathematical certainty but rather upon informed faith. "I began to realize that I believed countless things which I had never seen or which had taken place when I was not there to see . . . and so much that I believed on the word of friends or doctors or various other people. Unless we took these things on trust, we should accomplish absolutely nothing in this life" (*Conf.,* 6.5). If such things had to be taken on trust, it occurred to him that Christian faith might have to be built upon trust of a similar kind.

All this was dawning upon him as week by week Monica continued to go to the cathedral with her prayers for her son and he went to the same cathedral to hear the preaching and teaching of Ambrose—and not only to hear his preaching and teaching but to observe the whole style of the bishop's life, which spoke of apostolic and godly dedication.

We know from both his *Confessions* and his letters just how very much the bishop's daily life impressed the young Augustine. He gives us, if we will piece it together, almost an icon for the daily life of a bishop living in the style of St. Ambrose in the fourth century. Apparently his day began early with devotions, after which he would celebrate and distribute the Holy Communion in his basilica. Then he would sit down at a table in his great hall and read and study the Scriptures with the great Greek commentaries open around him. He would also include in his regular reading Plato, whom he admired. Apparently the doors to his house were always open.

Augustine tells us that anybody could approach Ambrose and consult him "without being announced." If anyone sought his counsel, the bishop would leave his reading and give his attention instantly. Strangely, Augustine did not avail himself of that kind of extended counseling; he addressed only minor questions to the busy bishop, questions that did not take long to answer. Nevertheless, Ambrose came to know Augustine and would call to him when they met, telling him how fortunate he was to have such a remarkable mother!

The bishop, we are told, fasted five days of the week till the evening. When his one meal was over, he would sit down to work on his sermons and his books, writing everything with his own hand rather than using a secretary. In addition to all this, he cared for the poor, and—what may have teased Augustine more than anything else—he upheld in his own life and teaching the place of celibacy and continence.

Crisis and Conflict

BUT now the story turns inward. The supporting cast is assembled, each member with a part to play. Yet it is the turmoil and questioning within Augustine that brought him to his ultimate breaking point. At one level, he tells us how in Milan he was "eager for fame and wealth and marriage," but at another level he realized that he was now in his thirties and "still floundering" (*Conf.*, 6.11). Furthermore, the sycophantic nature of his relationship with the court sickened his inner integrity. "My misery was complete," he tells us, when he was preparing a speech in praise of the emperor, "intending that it should include a great many lies which would certainly be applauded by an audience who knew well enough how far from truth they were" (*Conf.*, 6.6).

As he was preparing this speech and walking along one of the streets in Milan, he noticed a beggar who somehow had had his fill of food and drink. The beggar was laughing and joking. The contrast between the contented and happy beggar and Augustine's own life and inner misery called him to turn to his companions and comment ruthlessly on his own predicament. "My ambitions had placed a load of misery on my shoulders and the further I carried it the heavier it became." The beggar had found a happiness that Augustine felt to be quite beyond his grasp. "For by all my laborious contriving and intricate manoeuvres I was hoping to win the joy of worldly happiness, the very thing which this man had already secured at the cost of the few pence which he had begged" (*Conf.*, 6.6). Augustine was not in his heart a rich, successful, and notable professor of rhetoric after all. He felt himself impoverished, poorer than the beggar whom he had beheld.

There could be no doubt that the inner turmoil was for Augustine now overshadowing all else. He was beginning to prefer the teaching of Christianity and he had certainly and finally left the fold of the Manichees. If he belonged anywhere on this philosophical spectrum, it was now among those who were termed at that time in history "the academics." Today we would use the word in its proper meaning—*agnostics*—to explain their position: they claimed that it was never possible to know for certain anything about metaphysics or reality.

The eleventh chapter of book six of Augustine's *Confessions* reads like the record of a hideous nightmare. He was plagued by voices from opposite corners offering contrary advice. They were reaching a crescendo of conflicting intensity for Augustine, who turned first this way and then that in response to their contesting claims upon his intellectual, moral, and spiritual life. "And I reasoned with myself in this way, my heart was buffeted hither and thither by winds blowing from opposite quarters."

Objectively and intellectually Augustine told himself that he was still trying to find the origin of evil. "Where then is evil? What is its origin? How did it steal into the world? What is the root or seed from which it grew?" (*Conf.*, 7.5). The questions persisted, and he was no longer content with the nonsense the Manichees had proposed as answers. Yet, Augustine was to discover, as he freely admits later, that the problem was of course not purely intellectual at all. The problem lay within him, and so the question itself was loaded before he asked it—clouded by the fact that he was asking it and clouded also by the way in which he was asking it. "I was trying to find the origin of evil, but I was quite blind to the evil in my own method of research" (*Conf.*, 7.5). The distortions were within, in what Augustine would call "the eyes of the heart," so that he could not even see the questions properly, let alone the answers.

There was a further complication. He had for a long time been influenced by astrology, and he still wondered if his problem might not be located in the stars. (There really is nothing new under the sun: today we are given to wonder if our problems might not be attributable to our genes, our parents, or our environment.) But at this point a friend, Firminus, arrived and asked Augustine to read his horoscope. Although Augustine did not refuse outright to do this, he found that his opinions were changing. Indeed, he concluded that he was "almost convinced that it was all absurd and quite meaningless" (*Conf.,* 7.6). Another small milestone had been reached. He was released, and he knew he was released, from what he frankly calls "the bondage of astrology" (*Conf.,* 7.7). Nevertheless the turmoil continued.

"My ideas were always changing, like the ebb and flow of the tide," Augustine reports (*Conf.,* 7.7). However, largely as a result of the influence of Ambrose's teaching, a whole part of him could by this stage say with confidence that "the path of man's salvation" is to be found in "Christ . . . our Lord, and in the Holy Scriptures, which are affirmed by the authority of [God's] Catholic Church." At least something was established in his mind, even though he was still "burning with anxiety to find the source from which evil comes" (*Conf.,* 7.7).

Still turning this way and that intellectually and spiritually, Augustine now began to follow Ambrose in exploring Platonism. The platonic philosophy and worldview helped him to heal the fragmented and dualistic approach he had received

at the hands of the Manichees. A fragmented, schizoid worldview that sought to break off the pure and the spiritual from the depravity of the earthly and the profane no longer made sense to Augustine. He was now reaching out to the more wholesome view of creation afforded by the metaphysics of Plato—a view totally alien to the Manichaean frame of mind.

This more whole view of the world came in turn to be reflected in a new interior wholeness. Augustine summarizes the genius of the Christian worldview in very important and telling words that mark another milestone in his pilgrimage: "I no longer wished for a better world, because now I was thinking of the whole of creation, and in the light of this clearer discernment, I had come to see that though the higher things are better than the lower, the sum of the whole creation is better than the higher things alone" (*Conf.,* 7.13). That represented a major breakthrough.

Yet, as the days and months went by, bringing him nearer the approaching crisis and breakdown, Augustine began to realize that he needed not merely education but salvation: it was in Holy Writ, not in philosophical books, that he would find the words of healing for which he was so earnestly searching. Above all, it was charity and love as revealed in the person of Jesus Christ that he needed rather than another ideology or a new philosophical abstraction. Indeed, he was astonished to be able to tell himself that he now loved God "and not some phantom" in his place. Nevertheless—and here was the continuing problem—he could not "persist in the enjoyment of God." In other words, with his mind and his lips he could confess God, but with his heart and his will he was not yet at home with God.

It was in the area of his sexual life that the issue focused for Augustine. He had told Alypius earlier in Milan that he "could not possibly endure the life of a celibate" because he felt himself "so firmly caught in the toil of sexual pleasure" (*Conf.,* 6.12). Here, of course, he resonates very clearly with the autobiographical experiences of St. Paul himself, whose writing now began to hold pride of place in Augustine's reading and study.

Augustine "seized eagerly upon the venerable writings inspired by [God's] Holy Spirit, especially those of the apostle Paul"—such as his statement in Galatians 5:17 that "The impulses of nature and the impulses of the spirit are at war with one another." At last Augustine was beginning to realize something of what such verses meant. He could say as well as St. Paul, "The good that I would I do not, and the evil that I would not, that I do—so help me God" (Rom. 7:19). Paul's story was very similar to that of Augustine, and the solution and healing that were to come to Augustine very shortly would come in much the same way that they came to the apostle of the Jews—not simply by intellectual wrestling but by divine and loving intervention, not by the injection of a new idea but by the loving presence of a new person.

The dilemma continued, though we know it was now focused more clearly, because Augustine was able to say, "I was quite sure that it was better for me to give myself up to your love than to surrender to my own lust. But while I wanted to follow the first course and was convinced that it was right, I was still a slave to the pleasures of the second" (*Conf.,* 8.5). He persisted in praying a prayer that has since become very well known: "Give me chastity and continence, but not yet" (*Conf.,* 8.7).

Convergence and Conversion

HAPPILY, events and people not of Augustine's own choosing began to overtake him and fire his imagination with stories and images that changed his whole perspective. In the first place, Augustine decided to go and see Simplicianus, the spiritual father of Ambrose. "Ambrose truly loved him like a father, for it was through him that he had received [God's] grace," Augustine tells us (*Conf.,* 8.2). The two men talked together, and Augustine told Simplicianus of his recent readings in the Platonists that had been translated into Latin by none other than Marius Victorinus, who had once been professor of rhetoric at Rome and who had been converted most wonderfully to Christianity before he died. The talk with Simplicianus achieved two things. It endorsed Augustine's understanding of Platonism as a philosophy in which "God and his Word are constantly implied." But Simplicianus went further and told Augustine all about the conversion to Christianity of Victorinus, "whom he had known intimately when he was in Rome."

As Simplicianus related his story about Victorinus, Augustine hung on his every word. The story is impressive by any standards, telling how a man well-known in public life, "of great learning, with a profound knowledge of the liberal sciences" became a Christian. "He had been master to many distinguished members of the Senate, and to mark his outstanding ability as a teacher, he had even been awarded a statue in the Roman forum—a great honour in the eyes of the world. He had always been a worshipper of idols" and had taken part fully in all the public rites and ceremonies associated with the national deities. Like Au-

Two murals by Bernozzo Gozzoli in the church of Sant' Agostino in San Gimignano.

Right, *Augustine arriving in Milan*
Below, *Augustine teaching*

Left, *a mosaic portrait of Ambrose in the Basilica di Sant' Anbrogio in Milan*

Above, *a stained glass window in the basilica in Hippo depicting Ambrose and Monica. Ambrose played a key role in fulfilling the promise another bishop had made to Monica: "It cannot be that the son of these tears should be lost" (Conf., 3.12).*

gustine, he had read his way through the great philosophers of the day until eventually, but still in private, he said to Simplicianus, "I want you to know that I am now a Christian." But to this Simplicianus had replied, "I shall not believe it or count you as a Christian until I see you in the Church of Christ." At this, Victorinus would laugh and say, "Is it then the walls of the church that make the Christian?" (*Conf.*, 8.2).

In truth, of course, Victorinus was afraid "of offending his proud friends who worshipped heathen gods." Yet it was not long before one day he asked Simplicianus if they could "go to the church. I want to be made a Christian."

Simplicianus instructed him "in the first mysteries of the faith and soon afterwards, to the wonder of Rome and the joy of the Church, he gave in his name to be reborn through baptism."

By this time, Augustine must have been on the edge of his chair waiting to hear the climax of the story—a story that spoke to his condition in more ways than one. Eventually the time came for Victorinus to make his profession of faith. Now at Rome, "those who are about to enter into your grace usually make their profession of faith in a set form of words which they learn by heart and recite from a raised platform in view of the faithful." But—and this was the telling point—although "the priests offered to allow Victorinus to make his profession in private, as they often did for people who seemed likely to find the ceremony embarrassing," Victorinus would have none of it. He was adamant, determined to confess his faith publicly for all to hear. "So when he mounted the platform to make his profession," there was a sudden hush as all waited to hear this great orator speak.

This time Victorinus did not speak the vain words of rhetoric; rather, it was a moment when the living Word spoke to the ears of the human heart words of grace and forgiveness—a Word which all need to hear. "He made his declaration of the true faith with splendid confidence" (*Conf.*, 8.2), Augustine was told, and very impressive such words must have been to one who was also a rhetorician, standing on the very edge of faith and new Christian life. Augustine tells us that "when your servant Simplicianus told me the story of Victorinus, I began to glow with fervour to imitate him" (*Conf.*, 8.5). Simplicianus also added that the profession of faith that Victorinus had made cost him his job under the emperor Julian.

After his meeting with Simplicianus, Augustine went to church whenever he could spare time from his work. He was regularly accompanied by Alypius, who was living in Augustine's household together with Nebridius, Monica, Adeodatus, and probably several others. But now the story intensifies. One day, during the summer of 386, a man named Ponticianus, a Christian "who held a high position in the emperor's household," paid an unexpected visit to Augustine. Nebridius was not there at the time.

Having been received by Augustine and Alypius, Ponticianus "happened to notice a book lying on a table used for games" near where Augustine and Alypius were sitting. "He picked it up and opened it and was greatly surprised to find that it contained Paul's epistles" (*Conf.*, 8.6). Augustine volunteered the information that by this time he was in fact studying "Paul's writings with the greatest attention." The conversation then took a fresh turn. Ponticianus began to tell Augustine and Alypius about Antony, an Egyptian monk who had died thirty years previously, leaving behind disciples whose ranks were rapidly growing in number and influence throughout the church. All this was news to Augustine and Alypius. Apparently there was even a monastery right there, just outside the walls of Milan under the care of none other than the good bishop Ambrose.

Ponticianus went on to tell in very moving terms how he and a friend had been deeply influenced by the witness of the monastic life, particularly during the course of a visit with the emperor to a monastery at Treves. There they had encountered some monks living a life of simplicity and chastity and had discovered a copy of the life of St. Antony. Upon reading that life, they had experienced a real summons to imitate St. Antony in holiness of life while also experiencing a divine discontent with the affairs and success of this world.

"But while he was speaking, O Lord," writes Augustine in his *Confessions,* "you were turning me around to look at myself. For I had placed myself behind my own back, refusing to see myself. . . . All the time that Ponticianus was speaking my conscience gnawed away at me . . . , and when he had finished his tale and completed the business for which he had come, he went away, and I was left to my own thoughts. I made all sorts of accusations against myself. I cudgelled my soul and belaboured it with reasons why it should follow me now that I was trying so hard to follow you. But it fought back. . . . My inner self was a house divided against itself" (*Conf.,* 8.7-8).

The Garden in Milan

Now the crisis was reaching its climax. "There was a small garden attached to the house where we lodged. . . . I now found myself driven by the tumult in my breast to take refuge in this garden, where no one could interrupt that fierce struggle, in which I was my own contestant, until it came to its conclusion" (*Conf.,* 8.8).

"I tore my hair and hammered my forehead with my fists," Augustine tells us; "I locked my fingers and hugged my knees" (*Conf.,* 8.8). In that garden on that summer's day in 386, Augustine "probed the hidden depths" of his soul. At last, almost like an alcoholic, he was beginning to acknowledge his utter powerlessness to make the total offering of his life; he was beginning to acknowledge his divided will, of which his lust and incontinence were the obvious and apparent symptoms. He was always intending to be chaste—but always tomorrow. "How long shall I go on saying 'tomorrow, tomorrow'? Why not now? Why not make an end of my ugly sins now?" (*Conf.,* 8.12).

Suddenly "a great storm broke within me, bringing with it a great deluge of tears." He stood up and left Alypius, so that he "might weep and cry to his heart's content." He flung himself "down beneath a fig tree and gave way to the tears . . . when all at once I heard the sing-song voice of a child in a nearby house." And so in this most dramatic chapter of his spiritual autobiography, Augustine takes up the story in the first person.

Whether it was the voice of a boy or a girl I cannot say, but again and again it repeated the refrain "Take it and read, take it and read." At this I looked up, thinking hard whether there was any kind of game in which children used to chant words like these, but I could not remember ever hearing them before. I stemmed my flood of tears and stood up, telling myself this could only be a

divine command to open my book of Scripture and read the first passage on which my eyes should fall. For I had heard the story of Antony, and I remembered how he had happened to go into a church while the Gospel was being read and had taken it as a counsel addressed to himself when he heard the words Go home and sell all that belongs to you. . . . *So I hurried back to the place where Alypius was sitting, for when I stood up to move away I had put down the book containing Paul's Epistles.*

Augustine seized the book, opened it, and read the first passage that leapt from the page to his eyes. The passage that spoke to him was straight from Paul's epistle to the Romans: "Not in revelling and drunkenness, not in lust and wantonness, not in quarrels and rivalries. Rather, arm yourselves with the Lord Jesus Christ." Once again here is a case of the words of Scripture being the vehicle for the living Word of healing and salvation. The living Word of God was present and powerful for Augustine through the words of Scripture.

"I marked the place with my finger or by some other sign and closed the book," he went on. "My looks now were quite calm as I told Alypius what had happened to me. . . . Then we went in and told my mother, who was overjoyed." Again, what understatement he is given to! All those years— nearly thirty-three in all—of the prayers and entreaties of a mother had not gone unanswered after all. In his record of the event, Augustine immediately associates his conversion with the prayers of Monica, himself relating it in the form of a prayer. "For she saw that you had granted her far more than she used to ask in her tearful prayers and plaintive lamentations. You converted me to your-

self, so that I no longer desired a wife or placed any hope in this world but stood firmly upon the rule of faith, where you had shown me to her in a dream so many years before" (*Conf.,* 8.12).

So it was that Augustine was converted from the man of words to a disciple of the Word. In a moment, he tells us, "It was as though the light of confidence flooded into my heart and all the darkness and doubt was dispelled."

It is significant perhaps that the Roman Catholic Church celebrates in its calendar only two feasts of conversion—the one of St. Paul (January 25) and the other of St. Augustine (May 5). The two experienced similar and dramatic conversions, and they have been almost equally important in shaping the whole world of Christian thought, Catholic and Protestant alike. Augustine had his Damascus Road encounter in that garden in Milan. From that point onward there would be many times of backsliding, many failings and failures, but he had turned the corner and his life faced into a totally new and different perspective. In a real sense, he had reached a turning point in his life, and in his thirty-third year a new life was beginning.

CHAPTER FIVE

RETREAT, REFLECTION, AND WRITING

Retreat from Milan

BY high summer of 386, tongues must have been wagging in Milan concerning the strange behavior of their young professor of rhetoric. There can be little doubt that to the world around him, beyond the circle of his immediate and close friends, Augustine was displaying all the classic symptoms of a total breakdown. He tells us himself that during the summer he developed "a weakness of the lungs"; he "found breathing difficult" and "had pains in the chest." Furthermore, his "voice was husky": he had become of all things a professor of rhetoric who was compelled to admit that he could no longer "speak for long at a time" (*Conf.*, 9.2)!

There were three more weeks left until the end of term, and Augustine believed he could scarcely "manage to endure to the end of this period." He admits he had lost all ambition to make money, and in any case now found his job and his career a total contradiction to his newfound faith. "Now that I had been redeemed by you, I had no intention of offering myself for sale again" (*Conf.*, 9.2). With typical hyperbole he now speaks of his professorship as "a chair of lies." One thing was clear: he had to get away from it all and start a totally new life.

Another professor and close friend, Verecundus, was most anxious about recent events in Augustine's life. He was concerned from the start about Augustine's health, though he also knew about the "newfound blessings" of the events in that garden. Although he was not yet a Christian,

he was married to a Christian and had deep sympathies with all that Augustine was experiencing.

Vacation time was approaching in the hot and humid Po Valley of Milan. It so happened that Verecundus owned a large country house at Cassiciacum, and although he could not himself spend time at the villa, he was very happy to make it available to Augustine and his household for as long as they might care to use it. (In fact, we know that Verecundus died the following year after having been received into the faith of the church on his deathbed.) Augustine did not resign from his professorial chair at this point, but as soon as the autumn vacation was over he notified the authorities in Milan that "they must find another vendor of words for their students." He gave two reasons: in the first place he was now a Christian and intended to be baptized, and in the second place he was far from well.

Cassiciacum and Community

FROM September of 386 to February of 387, Augustine retired to the country villa at Cassiciacum for a time of retreat, reflection, and writing. Cassiciacum is usually identified today as Cassago Brianza, just south of Lake Como, with the Alpine peaks on the far horizon, set amid chestnut trees, deep green woodlands, and, as Warren Thomas Smith notes, "the fragrance of mint and aniseed."

Autumn was approaching, and the colors were changing. This is the only opportunity we have to watch Augustine drawing breath, as it were, with space and time and geography permitting him to reflect upon both the natural world around him and the hidden world within him. Frequently he was to recall this blessed time in his life, down to the details of the autumn leaves with their deep colors of gold and saffron and the streams choked with the dying foliage of the longer summer days.

Marriage was behind him. We do not know who took care of all the embarrassment of breaking off the relationship with his prospective wife. Nor do we know in what way the latest mistress was dismissed. Perhaps Monica took care of these details herself—as indeed she took care of so many things, including the new household in Cassago.

It would seem that the new household afforded quite a merry party! Augustine and Alypius were there, of course, with Adeodatus. Nebridius could not join them, but Augustine's elder brother Navigius, his cousins Rusticus and Lastidianus, and two of his students, Trygetius and Licentius, both about sixteen years old, helped to make up the group. Licentius was Augustine's star pupil, the son of Romanianus, Augustine's lifelong benefactor. It seems only too fitting that Augustine should have dedicated the principal book he wrote during those balmy days spent at the foot of the Alps— *Contra Academicos*—to this patron. Apparently Romanianus had just lost a lawsuit and so was not free to join the house party, though there is evidence to suggest that he would not have attended even if he could have, because he did not approve of it.

Such a retirement from ambition and one's public career for the pursuit of creative leisure, writing, and reflection was very common among literary personalities during the days of the late empire. It was the ancient ideal in fact of *otium liberale,* a sort of cultured "early retirement." Indeed, that is how Augustine himself speaks of it, especially later in his life when as an old man he is reviewing all his writings. He speaks of this time after his conversion experience in the garden as constituting something of a Christian *otium.* Romanianus should have recognized what his young mentor was doing, though after all his years of financial support he might still have considered Augustine's resignation a wasted opportunity.

In any case, along the lines of a "lay monastery," the reading party withdrew from the intrigues, the heat, and the intensities of university and court life in Milan and gathered in their temporary home in its idyllic location at the foot of the Italian Alps. To this day, a visit to Cassago Brianza will take you back in imagination to that villa at Cassiciacum. Archeological remains uncovered in the village there take us back to the late days of the Roman Empire, and a strong tradition locates Augustine's Cassiciacum on this very site. The villa that was situated there when Verecundus owned it was already quite old, intended as a kind of summer house for those times in the year when the heat and humidity of Milan would become overbearing. Over the years it had been renovated and enlarged. For example, we know that it had baths that were doubtless a real pleasure to Augustine and his company. He tells us how they used to gather there and hold their philosophical discussions.

And so they passed the balmy days of the fading summer of 386 with Monica presiding and plentifully providing for her extended family. That is not to say that she herself did not take a conspicuous part in their somewhat intense and rather self-conscious philosophical discussions. We know that Licentius sang the newly pointed psalms to the Ambrosian chant that he had heard and learned by heart in Milan. Unfortunately (at least from Monica's point of view), he insisted on singing these while seated on the lavatory! We are told of how the boys one day found a centipede, chopped it up, and then all gathered round to see how all the parts continued to move independently even after its dissection. This gave rise to a mighty metaphysical debate. Navigius, who had a bad liver, frequently found himself at odds with his younger brother's newfound faith. And, of course, Monica, as awesome as ever, spent her time organizing the meals and the household in general, while always ready to intervene with a well-chosen word at both appropriate and inappropriate moments.

It was in this kind of community *otium* that Augustine flourished and began to reflect and write. His reflections led him to the psalms, and his writings led him to begin long years of service with the pen. As he tells us in one of his later letters, "I endeavor to be one of those who write by progressing and who progress by writing" (*Epistolae,* 143.2). That was to be true, in fact, for the rest of his life.

Writings in Cassiciacum

T HE principal book he completed during the month of November in that year was *Contra Academicos.* His newfound faith led him to reject the skepticism and agnosticism of the academics. He contended to the contrary that through authority and reason, man can indeed attain to certitude. We need not spend all our days lost in uncer-

tainties and mere speculation. As a Christian, Augustine found the authority that would work together with reason mainly in Scripture, tradition, and the teachings of the church. Revelation had replaced mere speculation for him. *Contra Academicos* is a short work written in the form of a discussion between some of the principal characters who were staying in that villa—primarily Augustine, Licentius, and Trygetius. There is no doubt that throughout the written record of their discussions it is Licentius who plays the leading role (after Augustine of course!).

A second book was occasioned by Augustine's birthday—November 13. "It was consummated," he tells us, "during a three-day conversation." *De Beata Vita* ("Concerning Happiness") shows that already at this stage of his pilgrimage Augustine is quite adamant that happiness can be found only in the knowledge of God.

He wrote these two books and the scrap of another—*De Ordine*—in the setting of endless discussions in those happy and relaxed autumn weeks at Cassiciacum in 386. As Augustine himself testifies, "really great things, when discussed by little men, can usually make such men grow big" (*Contra Academicos,* 1.2.6). Clearly, from this point on Augustine maintained that philosophy and metaphysics are not exclusively the property of the professionals in the universities. Such matters go right to the heart of all men and women providing they are willing to seek the truth. The church is the environment in which such men and women earnestly seek the truth, whether or not they belong to the intelligentsia. Augustine would always contend that the church ought not to be a galaxy of intellectuals but rather a community seeking to live the life of truth—and it is more likely to apprehend that

Opposite page, *a stained glass window in the basilica in Hippo depicting Augustine's conversion in the garden in Milan*

Modern site of Cassiacum, just south of Lake Como, where Augustine spent the period from September 386 to February 387 reflecting and writing. He was to recall this blessed time often throughout the remainder of his life—especially the lush flora of the waning summer and autumn.

truth in discussions and in the fellowship of the church than in solitary abstract speculation. Yet Augustine keeps a balance in these emphases; he does not condemn either intellectual pursuits or solitary speculation. He urges the community to explore their newfound faith by what he calls "playing at philosophy" together, and he also insists that the learning program include plenty of space and time to be "with themselves" for the purpose of ruminating and thinking. There must be right respect in all of us for our own powers of reflection, by which we also learn the really deep and important things of life. We need to develop what Augustine would call our *ingenium.*

As the winter days drew on and the shadows crept in upon him, Augustine wrote yet another book—*Soliloquies.* It was his "first intimate self-portrait" (he completed it some years before he wrote his fuller autobiographical work, the *Confessions*), consisting of an extended argument between his reason and his soul. The work begins with an extended prayer to God containing a wonderfully worded passage that is still used frequently hundreds of years later:

> *Oh God, from whom to be turned is to fall;*
> *To whom to be turned is to rise;*
> *From whom to depart is to die;*
> *To whom to return is to revive;*
> *In whom to dwell is to live*
> *Whom no man loses unless he be deceived,*
> *Whom no man seeks unless he has been*
>   *admonished,*
> *Whom no man finds unless he has been purified.*
> *Whom to abandon is to perish,*
> *To reach out to whom is to love,*
> *To see whom is true possession.*
>
> —Soliloquies, *1.3*

Augustine's reflections on his hidden and inner life in the *Soliloquies* suggest the influence of the longer nights and shorter days of winter, a withdrawal from outside pursuits and movement toward the inner light and warmth of the hearth and the heart. For Augustine, the momentous year of 386 was drawing to a close and even the seasons around him seemed to indicate an inner winter's death of the old Augustine—a death that would demand as surely as it prepared for a spring of resurrection, a new life and new beginnings. There was only one place to find that new life, as Augustine knew only too well: in the waters of baptism and at the hands of Ambrose back in Milan. It was there that all things would be made new.

He had written to Ambrose when he terminated his contract in Milan, asking the bishop to advise him on which books of Scripture it would be best for him to study, so that he "might be better prepared and more fitted to receive" the sacrament of baptism (*Conf.,* 9.5). Ambrose had recommended the prophet Isaiah, but Augustine found the opening chapter somewhat difficult to understand and so he laid it aside for the time being.

In any event, the time of retreat at Cassago was drawing to a close, as the season approached to enroll in Ambrose's school in preparation for the approaching Lent—February 387.

Preparation for Baptism in Milan

APART from emergency situations, all adults seeking baptism in the fourth-century church in Milan would receive the sacrament on Easter morning—the Feast of the Resurrection.

Easter A.D. 387 came as late as it possibly can—April 24/25. It was as though the tardiness of the holy day that year reflected the somewhat reluctant and late surrender of Augustine in his quest for faith.

Augustine was to be joined by his friend Alypius and also by his son, Adeodatus, who was now in his mid-teens—a boy endowed, we gather, with much of the intelligence and fervor that his father so openly displayed. So it was that the three A's would enroll in a class as *competentes* and begin Lent that year with the prospect of six weeks of intense and rigorous instruction and preparation for their baptism—that foundational sacrament of the Christian church. For Ambrose, this was the peak of his year's teaching program, and he took personal responsibility for making sure that each candidate received full and faithful instruction in the mysteries of the Christian religion.

It was an awesome business. The church in those early decades after the peace of Constantine found itself surrounded by pagan religions, witchcraft, sorcery, and various ill-sorted superstitions. Yet it was also a season in the history of the church when many were coming forward to seek baptism; there were at that time almost more than the church could cope with, especially in Milan. Many of the competentes, not unlike Augustine himself, had dabbled with these other religions and cults. In that situation, the church sought to keep its mysteries of prayer and the sacraments and even the Scriptures themselves as untainted as possible from the surrounding smorgasbord of alternative religions and superstitious options.

At various points on the long and arduous course leading up to Easter, the various mysteries were passed on to the competentes solemnly and sacramentally during the principal liturgies throughout Lent. The handing over of the Lord's Prayer, the four Gospels, and other ingredients of Christian faith and practice were carefully and powerfully enacted amidst constant and solemn warnings against false doctrine, heresy, and schism. This was all undertaken by the bishop himself, who was principally active and responsible in his diocese for the continuation of unity of doctrine and practice through his powerful preaching and teaching.

The bishop was custodian and defender of the faith once handed over to the apostles. He was, if you like, the prime minister of word and sacrament, and he would delegate this responsibility to his priests only when he himself could not personally be present. As the centuries wore on, the bishop's colors were to become distinctive. The purple that was adopted in the later medieval era was in fact a perversion, an unfortunate attempt on the part of the episcopacy to ape the powers of the emperors. In Ambrose's time, however, the bishop's color was green. It was, after all, supremely the bishop who ministered the rites of initiation (baptism and confirmation); if he were doing his job as it should be done, he would never be very far away from those waters of baptism from which new life breaks out in a spring-like green of new vigor, new faith, and new fertility.

All this symbolism and all of Ambrose's labors were focused on the eve of Easter, when, in the shadows of the baptistry and the bright lights of the cathedral church, winter would finally give way to spring in Milan as surely as night gives way to dawn and darkness yields to light. The cry of the church at that Easter dawn would be "The light of Christ!"

The Basilica Nova had been built by Ambrose and dedicated as the Cathedral of the Holy Apostles. (The present church of St. Ambrogio stands close to the site of Ambrose's original basilica, which was subsequently destroyed—although the baptistry in which Augustine was baptized has recently been most wonderfully excavated.) Conveniently for Ambrose, he had also managed to find at just the right moment on opening his new cathedral and dedicating it the relics and bodies of two martyrs with which to consecrate his wonderful new edifice. A "certain burning feeling" convinced him that somehow some such relics would be given, and, after only a short time of searching, the complete and undefiled bodies of the martyrs St. Gervasius and St. Protasius were unearthed. Augustine tells us that on June 17, 386, the bodies "were carried to Ambrose's basilica with the honor that was due to them." Their bodies were sealed in the great sarcophagus beneath the high altar of the new basilica in the belief that holiness has a geography and is embodied (on the principle of the Incarnation) more in some places than in others and more in some people than in others. It is saints who make the church (building) holy, not the other way around.

Such had been the events in the new basilica in the "bumper" year of 386. Yet if 386 had been a good year for the basilica in Milan and for Ambrose, then 387 would prove to be the bumper year of years—for within its very walls our saint was to be baptized.

Easter Eve, A.D. 387: New Life

CROWDS were gathered there in the basilica on Easter eve to keep vigil and watch in readiness for the dawning of the new Easter day in the year of grace 387. We know that the crowds were there that night, because the closing years of the fourth century belonged to the sturdy days of Christianity—a faith that in those days still made demands upon its adherents.

Christianity was at last freed from the shackles of martyrdom and persecution. Initially this had strengthened the church, though in later years the newfound freedom and popularity proved to have less desirable consequences. Later generations were to tame the great sacrament of baptism almost out of recognition and make it just part of the domesticated decoration of the Christian way of life. But not so in Milan and certainly not while the resilient and ebullient Ambrose was bishop in the heroic concluding years of the fourth century.

Make no mistake about it, baptism at that time, in that place, and administered by those hands was an awe-inspiring rite. It borrowed every conceivable symbol of light and darkness, of water and fire, of oil and salt, of word and action, of life and death itself to impress once and for all upon the recipients of this great and glorious gift the eternal significance of this momentous turning point in their lives.

The drama began at midnight, as the vigil service of Easter eve gave place to the celebration of Easter day. Augustine, Alypius, and Adeodatus, together with their fellow competentes, had been fasting for three days before this great ceremony. From the time the sun set until midnight or even later, there were readings, psalms, and prayers. Then in the darkened church, in front of the high altar, the crowd of men and women seeking baptism knelt in silence. Bishop Ambrose, assisted by acolytes, deacons, and deaconesses, stepped forward and touched each new Christian on the ears

A mural by Benozzo Gozzoli in San Gimignano depicting Augustine's baptism. Baptism in that time and place was an awe-inspiring rite, employing a rich tapestry of symbolism to underscore the profundity and majesty of this momentous turning point in one's life.

and nostrils with spittle. The words rang out throughout the great cathedral: "*Epheta*—that is, be opened into the odor of sweetness." On this night of all nights, the basilica was packed to capacity with those who (like Monica) almost seemed to exist solely for the church—though it was also, on this night of all nights, a home for the wayward, the weak, and the erratic: the church exists for them as well.

Of course we may be sure that, as always in that congregation, Monica had taken her place. This moment was her life's goal. Humanly speaking, there can be no doubt that history was made on that night largely through her prayers and her tears and her intercessions. At last, Augustine was to be a true Christian. She had yielded her very lifeblood at his first birth; now she doubtless shed tears of love and joy as she was present (almost like a spiritual midwife) at his second birth. She had not been very far away at any step of the journey, and it is singularly fitting that she should have been present on this most holy night.

Yes, Easter came as late as possible that year, almost as though Augustine could not possibly have held off his commitment much longer. He did not know it then, but had he postponed it any longer, even just another year, it would have been too late—at least for Monica. It was to be her last Easter on earth. The resurrection she was sacramentally celebrating that night she would be experiencing through her own death only a matter of weeks later. Ends and beginnings were strangely overlapping and interwoven on that night. The baptistry in Milan on that occasion was in more ways than one representative of intersection—the end of the old, and the beginning of the new. What a way to end life; what a death through which to find life.

The baptistry in Milan was separate from the main building of the new basilica but could be approached from the main church under cover. Now the congregation had begun to sing one of the psalms they had recently learned specifically for this moment in the great baptismal liturgy. "As the hart desireth the water brooks, so longeth my soul after thee, O God." Yes, that was surely true in Augustine's case: his whole life had been a longing and a yearning for God. That yearning had been at the heart of all his earliest and most confusing experiences. He was to write the famous words at the opening of his *Confessions* some years later, "Thou hast made us for thyself and our hearts are restless till they rest in thee" (*Conf.*, 1.1). Although friendship and love had given to him their most generous moments, they had left him far from satisfied, had in fact only compounded the yearning and longing they were powerless to fulfill.

There had always been in Augustine a restlessness, even when love had been most accommodating, when love and lust had conspired together to give most richly of their bounty—still he had felt cheated. It was as though they made promises they could not keep, as though they could at best merely masquerade as envoys to something and someone else beyond them. All his best experiences of beauty and love were after all no more than what C. S. Lewis has described as "the scent of a flower we have not yet found, the echo of a tune we have not yet heard, news from a country we have never yet visited." For it was that yearning, that deeply unsatisfied desire, that panting which had brought Augustine to the point of breakdown during the summer of the previous year.

There had always been a restlessness and a sense of journeying in his life. As he was to write many years later, "Behold you were within me and I outside; and I sought you outside. . . . You were with me, and I was not with you. You called and cried to me and broke open my deafness; and you sent forth your beams and shone upon me and chased away my blindness; you breathed fragrance upon me, and I drew in my breath and now do pant for you: I tasted you and now hunger and thirst for you: you touched me, and I have burned for your peace."

And so the procession made its way from the basilica into the tomb-like baptistry. Augustine was at last coming home. The restless heart had at last found its only true and lasting peace.

The baptistry was octagonal in shape, not unlike the private baths, or *thermae,* in the houses of the very rich. In the center of the baptistry were three rows of steps leading concentrically down to a central pool. These steps at the bottom of the pool were beautifully and colorfully decorated with fine mosaics depicting, among other things, little fish. An earlier Christian teacher (Tertullian, also from Augustine's home country) had spoken most eloquently of the new Christians in those waters of the baptistry as being like little fish who together with their great fish *(Ichthys),* Jesus Christ, "were born again in water." Over the top of the bath area was a large baldachino supported by four tall pillars bearing up the roof of the pool, and between the pillars there were curtains—drawn open and readily inviting those who sought baptism to step down into the running waters and be immersed and drenched in the overwhelming love of God. Around the edge of the baptistry ran a corridor blazing with lamps where each of the candidates would strip, sit in the niches of the wall, and await the climax of the night's vigil—their baptism into the death and resurrection of Jesus Christ.

The bishop, for whom there was a special seat in the wall next to the pool, presided as Augustine, Alypius, and Adeodatus in turn went down into the tomb of baptism and were subsequently raised from the womb of new life as neophytes, new Christians, born again in the waters of regeneration. The waters for the ceremony of baptism had to flow freely in those days, because stagnant water (especially in hot countries) could only be the bearer of corrupted life. So here indeed was a river, and the prayers and preparations for this holy night had led these new Christians (and all the old ones, too, seeking in their turn renewal and refreshment) to the point of crossing that river.

No one was under any illusions. All of them were in some sense Red Sea Christians, delivered at last from slavery and bondage as they went from the baptistry back into the church to be fed with manna, the food they would need as they set out on their pilgrimage toward the land of promise and peace. The imagery at every point was so powerful as to be almost overwhelming. Fire and water, birth and death, old and new, womb and tomb—imposing contradictions and paradoxes, impossible to take in and comprehend entirely, yet powerful in their impact on the mind, the imagination, the heart; above all, they were able to melt and refashion the steel of the human will, twisted as it is by sin. There was no lecture or exhortation—none of the seduction of rhetoric with which Augustine and Ambrose were both so familiar. It was as though the words now trailed behind the actions, running to keep up and already clearly out of breath as Bishop Ambrose, like a sort of latter-day Moses, led his new Christians back to his new basilica for the climax of the Eucharist—the first Eucharist of Easter Day A.D. 387.

A baptistry in Djemila showing the niches in which the candidates sat during the night awaiting their baptism into the death and resurrection of Jesus Christ

The steps leading down into the pool in which the immersion took place

Above, *a stained glass window in the basilica in Hippo depicting Ambrose baptizing Augustine*

Left, *a close-up view of the floor around the baptistry pool shown on the opposite page. Tertullian likened new Christians in the baptismal waters to little fish who, together with the great fish, Jesus Christ, "were born again in water."*

A New Beginning

FOR the next week, Augustine, Adeodatus, and Alypius, dressed in their white robes of chrism, attended the basilica each day to make their communion and to hear Ambrose round off his school of instruction with additional magnificent scriptural sermons and teaching. The new life had begun. Looking back on the remaining weeks spent in Milan (which he was never again to visit), to the time spent with Ambrose (whom he was never again to see), from the vantage point of later life as a bishop himself—the "Ambrose" of Hippo—Augustine was to write that

> We were baptized, and all anxiety over the past melted away from us. The days were all too short, for I was lost in wonder and joy, meditating upon your far-reaching providence for the salvation of the human race. The tears flowed from me when I heard your hymns and canticles, for the sweet singing of your Church moved me deeply. The music surged in my ears, truth seeped into my heart, and my feelings of devotion overflowed, so that the tears streamed down. But they were tears of gladness.
> —Conf., 9.6

Just before his baptism, Augustine had started a book that he was later to complete in Africa in 389. In this work, *De Musica* (perhaps inspired by the music of the liturgy of the cathedral in Milan), he discusses rhythm, meter, and verse. However, it is not primarily about music as we understand it; it is more metaphysical in implication, seeking out the numbers and rhythm of the universe—a sort of cross between mathematics, physics, and the music of the spheres!

By this time, still in Milan, the Augustine household had very much become a community and a sort of monastic cell. Alypius had thoroughly committed himself to his new way of life. During the few months it spent back in Milan in 387, the African caucus was joined by another North African (also from Thagaste, as a matter of fact)—Evodius, another recent convert. He had formerly been an employee of the government in the secret police force, but he took early retirement intending to withdraw from the world and live out his Christian discipleship within the environment of community.

After long discussions, Augustine and his household decided they could best serve God as a community established back in Africa—or, more specifically, in Thagaste, where it had all begun. Roots are strong and frequently reclaim our allegiance in later life, pulling us back whence we originated. So it was to be with Augustine and his band of merry men together with Monica.

In one way, they could not have chosen a worse moment to set out on their long journey homeward to Africa. Civil war in Italy was pending as the brutal General Maximus prepared to invade. He was blockading all the harbors of Rome, and so when the African party arrived in Ostia (at the mouth of the Tiber), there was no hope of finding a ship free to set sail on the two-day journey back to Carthage. Normally there would have been plenty of merchant ships setting sail on that journey and many others. Augustine knew well the streets where the shipping merchants were housed (as do we, for they are still clearly marked to this day), but just when he most needed such transportation there was none to be had. He was compelled to remain in Italy for almost a year.

The Vision in Ostia

On arriving in Ostia, they were given housing by prominent and wealthy Christians who were members of the nobility. Such rich and prominent Christians were not rare in the empire; indeed, the wealthiest family in the empire, the Anicii family, was Christian. Among the many palaces and houses of this wealthy class there would surely be room and hospitality for Augustine and his strange little African party.

But where they were housed in Ostia is irrelevant. The important features of Augustine's enforced stay in Ostia are not to be found in his housing but in the momentous events that occurred during his stay. First of all, as Augustine reports, "While we were at Ostia, at the mouth of the Tiber, my mother died" (*Conf.*, 9.8).

Of course, we need to realize that the only account of Monica's death and the time she spent with her son at Ostia comes to us directly from the pen of Augustine himself, retrospectively recounted and necessarily romanticized and idealized. Nevertheless, on any showing, her death and the events surrounding it were as distinctive and spiritually significant as her entire life had been.

Augustine describes for us a conversation he had with his mother just two weeks before her sudden death in Ostia. They spoke while "leaning from a window which overlooked the garden in the courtyard of the house where we were staying in Ostia" (*Conf.*, 9.10). They were waiting in that house, clearly rather a grand one, after their "long and tiring journey, away from the crowd" so that they could be refreshed for the sea voyage and the next leg of their journey homeward to Africa. It

appears that their conversation was serene and joyful. Clearly son and mother were now, since Augustine's conversion and baptism, very much on the same wavelength. They resonated with each other in their conversation and in sharing their experiences of the spiritual and the inner life. Their conversation, which began with their sharing deep inner experiences of the spirit, ended in what history has become compelled to regard as a kind of vision.

"As the flame of love burned stronger in us," Augustine tells us, "and raised us higher towards the eternal God, our thoughts ranged over the whole compass of material things in their various degrees, up to the heavens themselves, from which the sun and the moon and the stars shine down upon the earth." Their conversation quickened in pace and gathered in intensity.

Higher still we climbed, thinking and speaking all the while in wonder at all that you have made. At length we came to our own souls and passed beyond them to that place of everlasting plenty. . . . There life is that Wisdom by which all these things that we know are made, all things that ever have been and all that are yet to be. . . . And while we spoke of the eternal Wisdom, longing for it and straining for it with all the strength of our hearts, for one fleeting instant we reached out and touched it.
—Conf., *9.10*

It was clearly one of those moments of divine disclosure that are difficult if not impossible to describe in words, precisely because we are taken beyond words and images into a contemplative experience that by its very nature can be neither described nor defined.

A stained glass window in the basilica in Hippo depicting the vision Monica and Augustine had while staying in Ostia. "And while we spoke of the eternal Wisdom, longing for it and straining for it with all the strength of our hearts, for one fleeting moment we reached out and touched it" (Conf., 9.10).

Those infused with the cynicism and reductionism of the twentieth century scarcely know what to make of such an event or the highly charged and deeply personal description Augustine gives of it. As T. S. Eliot notes, "Human kind cannot bear very much reality." We are always in danger of indulging in either romanticism or cynicism. Many of the artists who have attempted to depict this scene of Augustine and Monica at the window have fallen into the former, whereas most serious and scholarly discussions of the event have fallen into the latter.

Surely we are dealing here with what one writer calls "the doors of perception." It could be that earlier ages schooled in Christian prayer knew better than most know today just how to open those doors, knew how to receive a gift of vision beyond the finite framework of our contemporary mindset. Imprisoned within rationalism, our contemporary world still yearns for the vision of what is beyond. We have all been created for such a vision. Deprived of contemplation, meditation, and the release of transcendent worship, our age turns to drugs and transcendental meditation techniques. In the vision he shared with his mother only a matter of days before the end of her life, Augustine was pointing appropriately in this context of the imminence of death to the chief end and purpose of mankind—namely, that we are "created in order to worship God and to enjoy him forever."

At the conclusion of their time together, Monica turned to face Augustine. She had a word now for him:

My son, for my part I find no further pleasure in this life. What I am still to do or why I am here in the world, I do not know, for I have no more to hope for on this earth. There was one reason, and one alone, why I wished to remain a little longer in this life, and that was to see you a Catholic Christian before I died. God has granted my wish and more besides, for I now see you as his servant, spurning such happiness as the world can give. What is left for me to do in this world?

—Conf., *9.10*

Death of Monica

Monica's words were true—true in ways that neither of them might have realized fully at the time. She had lived for and prayed for Augustine since the day of his birth, and her prayers had been answered more wonderfully than she could possibly have envisaged. But now no motivation remained; she could see no point to a life lived without purpose, or with a purpose that could be achieved only beyond the barrier of death.

"It was about five days after this, or not much more, that she took to her bed with a fever" (*Conf.,* 9.11). She went into a coma for a time, but on recovery immediately asked to see Augustine. To the end, Monica was in control. "You will bury your mother here," she said. Augustine, trying to hold back the tears, made no reply.

It was Navigius, the elder brother, who was quick to protest. He wished for Monica's sake that she could die in her own country and not abroad. His sentiment did not please Monica. She turned to her younger son, her favorite son, and spoke rather disparagingly of Navigius's very natural concerns for her. "See how he talks!" she said to Augustine. Then, facing them both, she made her wishes clear.

"It does not matter where you bury my body," she said quite plainly. "Do not let that worry you! All I ask of you is that, wherever you may be, you should remember me at the altar of the Lord." And the church has never ceased to do so, on St. Monica's Day each year, fittingly enough the day before the church observes the Feast of Augustine's conversion—May 4.

Soon she hardly had the strength to speak. Her illness grew daily worse, and "she was in great pain."

"And so," Augustine concludes, "on the ninth day of her illness, when she was fifty-six and I was thirty-three," she died (*Conf.,* 9.11). The deathbed scene was indeed painful for Augustine. "I closed her eyes," he tells us, "and a great wave of sorrow surged into my heart." With great effort, he held back the tears for later, while Adeodatus "began to wail aloud." Augustine had the comfort of knowing from his mother's lips during the last stages of her illness that she had regarded him as being "a good son to her"; apparently she even went so far as to tell him that "she could not remember ever having heard me speak a single hard or disrespectful word against her" (*Conf.,* 9.12).

Adeodatus was calmed and reassured when Evodius, the new member of the community, began to sing Psalm 101—"My song shall be of mercy and justice"—and the rest of the community took up the responses around the deathbed.

Portion of Augustine's tomb in the church of San Pietro Ciel D'oro, Pavia, depicting the death of Monica. The work was created by the pupils of Giovanni Balducchio of Pisa in the fourteenth century.

"When the body was carried out for burial, I went and returned without a tear," reports Augustine. Nor did he weep during the Requiem Mass for Monica while the "body rested by the grave before it was laid in the earth," as was the custom in the Italian church at that time. He was too distraught for tears. He went to the baths, which were supposed to ease the mind by washing away anxiety. (Archeological work in Ostia has uncovered a Roman bath there bearing an inscription dating back to the time of Augustine and advertising a "soothing wash." We are able today to come very close to determining the path Augustine must have traveled through the streets of Ostia in his bereavement, to finding the very stones he eventually washed with his tears.) In the baths he found that the "water could not wash away" his bitter grief. That night in bed, he tells us, he recalled a hymn written by Bishop Ambrose and set to a melody that he had doubtless often sung in those memorable days in Milan. To this day the church still sings Ambrose's "Evening Hymn" at vespers.

Maker of all things! God most high!
Great Ruler of the starry sky!
Who, robing day with beauteous light
Hath clothed in soft repose the night.

That sleep the wearied may restore
And fit for toil and use once more;
May gently sooth the careworn breast
And lull our anxious griefs to rest.

Augustine's anxious griefs were slow to be healed, but recalling this hymn brought comfort to him in the night, and at last he was able, he tells us, "to weep for her and for myself and to offer" his tears to God for Monica's sake as well as for his own.

"The tears which I had been holding back streamed down, and I let them flow as freely as they would, making of them a pillow for my heart" (*Conf.*, 9.12).

Monica was buried in Ostia. In 1945, two boys playing in a small courtyard beside the Church of St. Aurea in that city were digging a hole to plant a post for a game they were playing and they uncovered a fragment of marble. It turned out to be Monica's tombstone, still bearing part of the original inscription.

Yet the inscription of Monica's love and prayers for Augustine were carved not on stone or marble but on the heart, in the life, and in the writings of that favorite son whose life she had so influenced. For the next forty years, until his own death in 430, he was also to inscribe upon the heart of the church and indeed upon our Western civilization the story of his great love affair with God—a love affair that began at his mother's knee.

The Journey Home to Africa

AUGUSTINE returned to Rome with Evodius to await the lifting of the blockade. After many attempts they were at last able to secure in Ostia a ticket to go with a shipping merchant on the two-day sailing journey back to Carthage. Augustine took Adeodatus with him, but this time the journey was made without either mother present—without Adeodatus's mother or Monica.

It was the end of the beginning, and there had been much accompanying bereavement. On the eve of his departure, Augustine also lost his good friend Verecundus, who had been so generous and so timely in offering the use of his house in Cassago. The baptism, of course, had also been a

*A sign on the Via della Corporazione in Ostia, the Roman seaport from which a grieving
Augustine departed to return to Carthage*

sort of death—a real break with the past, bringing the new Christians through that Red Sea on whose far shores alone new life can really begin.

We may hope that in the midst of all his various bereavements Augustine found some comfort during that crossing over to Carthage as he looked out at the sea. He loved the sea in a way that landlubbers frequently do, romantically projecting onto the waters a healing inner stream of tears and peace. Many years later he was to write in such a way about the sea. Although he did not like sea travel, it may not be too fanciful to suppose that such reflections originated during that nostalgic crossing, perhaps when he was alone on board or perhaps when he looked out at the huge expanse of water with its new horizons and changing perspectives. In any event, he was to write many years later of "the mighty spectacle of the sea . . . putting on its changing colours like different garments, now green, with all the many varied shades, now purple, now blue" (*De Civitate Dei, 22.24*).

Such reflections might well have accompanied him as he sailed back to his native country with his strange little African party of friends and family. It was St. Paul, that other great hero of the faith, who summarized such a time of change and development in his own life in words that most certainly applied to Augustine at this point in his life and pilgrimage: "Not that I have already obtained this or am already perfect; but I press on to make it my own, because Christ Jesus has made me his own. Brethren, I do not consider that I have made it my own; but one thing, I do, forgetting what lies behind and straining forward to what lies ahead, I press on toward the goal for the prize of the upward call of God in Christ Jesus" (Phil. 3:12-14).

So too with Augustine. The new life was only just beginning and all kinds of surprises and shocks awaited him on his return journey back to his motherland—for the first time in his life without his own mother, without a career, without a wife. The major part of his life still lay ahead of him, though now he faced it as a captive of Christ and a servant of God.

Opposite page, *a stained glass window in the basilica in Hippo depicting the death of Monica. "My son," she told Augustine in her last days, "I find no further pleasure in this life. . . . There was one reason, and one alone, why I wished to remain a little longer in this life, and that was to see you a Catholic Christian before I died. God has granted my wish and more besides" (Conf., 9.10).*

Right, *"The Vision," an oil painting in Pavia depicting the mystical experience Monica and Augustine shared after his baptism*

Below, *the courtyard of a grand home in Ostia similar to the one in which Augustine and his party stayed while waiting to return to Africa*

J. BESSAC à Grenoble

CHAPTER SIX

CHAINED TO THE GOSPEL

Carthage: A Miracle?

TOWARD the end of 388, Augustine arrived back on North African soil, doubtless docking not far from where he had escaped Monica's clutches and slipped his moorings for his momentous Italian pilgrimage some five years before. It is impossible to believe that many memories of his earlier life did not come flooding back to him as the ship drew near to Carthage. There is no reason to suppose that Carthage had changed very much since the days of his youth as a student or later as a teacher. Yet Augustine had changed dramatically. He was a new man in an old place, seeing it all from a very different perspective. As a matter of fact, during his years as bishop of Hippo he would visit Carthage many times to participate in controversial councils of the church.

It is not surprising that writing some years later he was to recall in significant detail the events surrounding this particular return visit to Carthage on his way back home to Thagaste. By this time, the little African group that had lived together informally in community had developed a more formal identity, had come to be known as *Servi Dei*—"Servants of God." As Peter Brown notes, "they owed their position in the Latin church less to any connection with an organized monastic life, than to the pressure of a fashion in perfection. They produced some of the most remarkable men of their time" (*Augustine of Hippo*, p. 132).

The Servants of God were what we today might call a lay order, living out the vows of baptism as dedicated and deeply committed Christian lay men and women. Alypius and Augustine and eventually the small retinue of the Servants of God were invited on arrival to stay temporarily in the home of Innocentius, "sometime counsellor of the vice-prefecture . . . a most devout man" (*De Civitate Dei,* 22.8), living in an equally devout household.

Years later, writing his magnum opus, the *City of God,* Augustine was to recall a miracle of healing granted in that household during the brief visit of the Servants of God. Innocentius, he tells us, "was under treatment for fistulas, having a number of them entwined in the rectum, and others more deep-seated. The surgeons had operated on some and were now proceeding with medical treatment; but the patient had suffered long-lasting and acute pain in the operation. Now there still remained one ulcer which had escaped the notice of the medical men, and it was so deeply hidden that they could not get at it, since it would require to be opened up by an incision" (*De Civitate Dei,* 22.8). Time passed, and Innocentius dismissed several surgeons from his home. Finally, a particularly famous "surgeon of genius" from Alexandria was duly sent for to perform this painful and unpleasant operation.

The evening before the operation was due to take place, Innocentius was visited by Bishop Saturninus (at that time bishop of Uzalis) and by a priest and deacons from the church. Innocentius was clearly terrified by the operation due to take place next day, so all turned to prayer—the good bishop, his deacons, the terrified Innocentius and the somewhat overawed and bewildered Augustine and the other Servants of God who were present. "We rose from our knees and, after receiving the bishop's blessing, we left, the sick man entreating his visitors to come back in the morning."

"The dreaded morning dawned." All were in attendance. "The servants of God arrived as they had promised; the surgeons entered. . . . The fearful instruments were produced, while we all sat there in dumbfounded suspense. . . . The bandages were untied; the place was bared. The surgeon examined it, and knife in hand ready for the incision, he searched for the fistula that was to be cut. He inspected it closely; felt it with his fingers; then he examined it in every way." Yes, it had healed, apparently miraculously in answer to prayer, and no operation was necessary. Doubtless it was not long before champagne corks were popping in the household of Innocentius on that momentous day, during the brief but memorable stay of the Servants of God in Carthage on their way back to Thagaste.

Thagaste—Further Bereavement

So the little group of the Servants of God returned to where it had all begun for Augustine. Alypius, Evodius, Severus, and Adeodatus were certainly in Augustine's little community by the time it arrived back in Thagaste, where they settled on a portion of Augustine's family estate. Nebridius was not with them, having returned to Africa; he was living with his mother in his country house near Carthage.

Separated though they were by distance, Nebridius and Augustine were united in their determination to live out their days in the pursuit of holiness. For such a lifestyle, space and quiet were essential. As Augustine wrote in a letter to Nebridius in Carthage, "I cannot taste and relish that true good unless a certain measure of carefree leisure falls to my lot. Believe me, a man does not achieve freedom from fear through his own insensibility, or boldness, or greed of empty glory, or superstitious credulity, but only by a considerable detachment from perishable things" (*Epistolae*, 10.2).

Correspondence between Carthage and Thagaste, between Nebridius and Augustine continued over the early months in their new life. "Your letters are as precious to me as my eyes," says Augustine in one of the many letters they exchanged. "For they are great, not in length, but in the subjects. . . . They speak to me of Christ, of Plato, of Plotinus" (*Epistolae*, 6.1).

Nebridius and Augustine were anxious to meet again, but neither could make the journey. Augustine at the best of times disliked traveling of any kind and pleaded that Nebridius should come over to Thagaste and settle with the community. "We can live here more satisfactorily than at Carthage, or even in the country." However, Nebridius could not in fact have made the journey whether he liked it or not. He was ill. Eventually he wrote and told Augustine about his illness, and shortly thereafter news arrived that he had died. It was yet another bereavement, another loss of friends and family.

Then, hard on the heels of this bereavement, Adeodatus suddenly died, at the age of eighteen. There can be no doubt that Augustine was genuinely fond of his only son, that he admired his growing intellectual abilities and was grief stricken on his sudden death. Now almost all of Augustine's family had gone—Patricius his father, Monica, his nameless concubine (whom so far as we know he never saw again on his return to Africa), Nebridius, and Adeodatus. Alypius was soon to become bishop of Thagaste and thus necessarily become more distant.

Augustine, approaching forty, was being stripped of many earthly ties. For someone who always needed people around him, such losses inevitably brought insecurity, though they brought a compensating clarity of focus to his aims and his ideals as well. He speaks of the insecurity in a letter: "That indeed, is something—to be stripped of vain cares and clothed with useful ones. But I doubt whether any security is to be hoped for in this world" (*Epistolae,* 18.1). Death had come suddenly and fiercely to Monica, Nebridius, and Adeodatus; there had been little chance to prepare or adapt.

Community Life and Study

BUT through his bereavement Augustine was, doubtless unconsciously, preparing and adapting for a future he could not possibly have foreseen. He was building upon the firmer foundation of a more structured community life, placing contemplation, study, and Scripture more to the forefront and shifting philosophy into second place. Since he was a layman, it does not seem likely that he was seeking ordination. But he was writing again; in 390 he produced another book, *On True Religion,* which he dedicated to his old friend and patron Romanianus.

In *On True Religion* Augustine is basically telling us that Christ has achieved what Plato sought in vain to do. Augustine is grateful to the philosophers, but in the end he knows that philosophy will not save the souls of men and women. All his writings are salted increasingly now with quotations from Scripture rather than the philosophers. (In fact he had deliberately left his textbooks behind when he returned to Africa: Scripture was now to be his principal textbook.)

Augustine made a special point of addressing

On True Religion to the Manichees, who flourished in Thagaste and indeed throughout the whole of North Africa. He sets out in full the Christian doctrine of the Fall, noting how it explains the presence of evil in the world. Needless to say, he condemns all the elaborate schemes and explanations of evil put forward by the Manichees and advocates Christian salvation in forthright and powerful phrases.

Augustine clearly realized that it was difficult for some of his former Manichaean friends to recognize him since his conversion—including his former friend Romanianus, who had much sympathy with the Manichaean philosophy. So toward the end of his book, the clarion call rings out in words that leave no place for apology or compromise: "One God alone I worship, the sole principle of all things, and his Wisdom who makes every wise soul wise, and his gift whereby all the blessed are blessed" (*On True Religion,* 55.112). This book was hailed by one notable contemporary as Augustine's "Pentateuch against the Manichees."

Yet in all of this, Augustine was still the restless heart. He spent his long life grappling with new challenges—which is perhaps why he lived so long and achieved so much. But he was no longer restless as he had earlier been at Thagaste, Carthage, Rome, or Milan. He experienced more the kind of restlessness we would associate with the pilgrim who refuses to settle for anything short of the ultimate goal. Increasingly he turned in the Scriptures to the Psalms and to St. John, books in which there is a quest for the face of God and a desire within the heart to ascend "to the fixed place" in the ascent of man. "Thither we make our way, still as pilgrims, not yet at rest; still on the road, not yet home; still aiming at it, not yet attaining it" (*Sermons,* 103).

92

Later he was to preach from such a questing and restless heart, but now hidden in Thagaste, already his days were numbered as a man of quiet, reflection, and hidden community life.

Hijacked in Hippo

EVER since Alypius had been seized upon for ordination to the episcopate as bishop of Thagaste, Augustine had deliberately avoided visiting any towns in which bishoprics were vacant, lest he himself should be snatched from a life of reflection and pushed into the life of a pastor and protagonist of the Christian church. But in 391 he had occasion to leave Thagaste for a visit to Hippo Regius on the north coast hard by the port of Annaba—a journey of some sixty miles. Hippo was very different from the town of Thagaste; among African cities it was in fact second in importance only to Carthage.

There were two reasons for Augustine's journey. He was to meet with a clerk of the imperial ministry of the interior who was toying with the idea of becoming a monk. Possidius, his biographer, tells us that the man "conceived a strong desire to see Augustine. . . . A report of this came to Augustine from a reliable source and he longed for this soul to be rescued from the dangers of this life and from eternal death. So without being asked, he went at once to the city, now so famous [Hippo] and saw the man. He had several talks with him and urged him, with all the force God gave him, to see that his promises to God were kept. The man kept promising from day to day to do this, but never carried it out during the visit of Augustine" (*The Life of St. Augustine,* 3). Nevertheless, this anonymous wan-

derer did more for the church of God than he could ever have imagined: he brought Augustine, the right man, to the right place at the right time, and events soon began to overtake all Augustine's well-laid plans.

Much later in life, in a sermon to his flock in Hippo, Augustine spoke of the second reason he made that fateful journey to their city: "I was looking for a place to set up a monastery, to live with my 'brethren.' I had given up all hope in this world. What I could have been, I wished not to be; nor did I seek to be what I am now" (*Sermons,* 355.2). Peter Brown has written that "when Augustine arrived in Hippo, in the spring of 391, he was a lonely man, entering middle age, who had lost much of his past and who was groping, half consciously, for new fields to conquer" (*Augustine of Hippo,* p. 137). Our restless saint was on the move again.

Possidius takes up the story where the questing Augustine arrived in Hippo:

At this time the office of bishop in the Catholic church in Hippo was held by that holy man Valerius. He was now impelled by the pressing needs of the church to address his flock and to impress upon them the necessity of finding and ordaining a priest for the city. The Catholics were by now aware of the holy Augustine's teaching and way of life, and they seized hold of him—he was standing in the congregation quite unconcerned and with no idea of what was going to happen to him. (While a layman, as he tried to tell us, he used to keep away from churches where the bishopric was vacant but only from these.) Holding him fast they brought him, as their custom was, to the bishop for ordination, for they were unanimous in asking for this to be done then and there. And while they were demand-

ing this with eager shouts, he was weeping copiously.

—The Life of St. Augustine, 8

Ordination by acclamation was quite the norm in the church at this time; many a passing "star" found himself "kidnapped" and raised to the office either of priest or bishop in the church of God. It had happened to Augustine's great hero Ambrose in 374, when the Christians in Milan had seized him and shouted, "Ambrose for bishop, Ambrose for bishop." Now it had happened to Ambrose's spiritual son, who was a layman at breakfast and a priest by lunchtime!

But Hippo was no showcase for the orthodox Christian minority under its aging and somewhat eccentric bishop Valerius. We are told that Valerius was "a Greek by birth and less versed in the Latin language and literature." But he was wise enough to know that he had found his man in Augustine. Manichaeism had taken hold very strongly in Hippo. As St. Paul the Jew had appeared at a time when Judaism needed to hear the challenge of Christianity, so it was that Augustine, the former Manichee, appeared when orthodox Christianity was embattled on all sides by heresies, Manichaean and otherwise.

Indeed, just across the street another sect posed its threat to Christian doctrine: the Donatists. They had their own bishop, a larger and a more prosperous congregation, and they could frequently be heard to "roar like lions" from their building only a block or so away from the cathedral in which the aging, Greek-speaking Valerius presided as bishop at the orthodox liturgy. But now there was Augustine, the new priest, outstandingly well-versed in Latin and rhetoric, totally at home with the Punic dialect of the country people in the diocese, well fitted by his experience with the Manichees to deal with this sect and beat them at their own arguments.

A Champion of the Gospel

IMMEDIATELY after his ordination, Augustine set up his monastery in Hippo, moving from Thagaste and requesting from Bishop Valerius space and time to give particular attention to studying the Scriptures in order to arm himself for the impending combat. He was to become in his lifetime a walking biblical concordance, commentary, and encyclopedia all rolled into one. He was to quote Scripture, we are told by one writer, no fewer than 42,816 times in all of his written works. His ordination had been no mean coup for the orthodox church in Hippo.

Little wonder that with such an eloquent and well-armed new presbyter on his staff, Valerius was prepared to break with a sacred tradition of the African church at that time and invite Augustine to preach frequently at the cathedral in his presence. That must have offended many who believed that it was the bishop and the bishop only who, as "prime minister" of the word, should sit on his cathedra and expound from Holy Scripture. Augustine had not been a priest five minutes—indeed he had not been a Christian for very much longer—and already this upstart was preaching on the basics of Christian belief before no less august a group than the assembly of the Catholic bishops from Africa who were convening in Hippo. Youth and brilliance do not sit easily together, and those in whom they do conjoin are seldom popular with their seniors. Nevertheless, Augustine was in a sense a professional in the art of public speaking, debate, and communication. Valerius had played a winning card in ordaining Augustine to the priesthood, and Augustine knew it.

Augustine effected changes at this point in his life that are in many ways most remarkable. From his ordination onward we see a highly skilled and articulate philosopher becoming a dedicated pastor and a patient protagonist for the Christian religion, apparently content to offer his energies and skills for almost the next forty years of his life amid the inefficiencies, ecclesiastical squabbles, and doctrinal divisions that were regrettably characteristic of the church in the North Africa of his day.

Valerius may well have been a holy man, but in leadership and in missionary zeal he left a great deal to be desired. The Donatist church was not only the largest church in Hippo, but it was also the church most conspicuously diligent in seeking to convert the outlying villages around Hippo and on the high ground beyond the river Seybouse. Falling in behind Valerius, Augustine soon found himself working as an ecclesiastical and legal lackey, rushing round pursuing lawsuits. It began to look as though the genuine missionary and evangelistic challenge of the church at Hippo was not going to be met: administration would once again displace ministry and mission.

The Manichees also had a very strong presence in Hippo under the leadership of their powerful and articulate priest Fortunatus, who had settled in the city and attracted many to that schismatic body. Fortunatus knew Augustine from their days in Carthage together. He had been unable to satisfy Augustine's intellectual demands at that time and so was most reluctant to accept Augustine's invitation for an open formal debate in the hall of a public bathhouse in Hippo. But the Manichees were thirsty for blood, and they pressed the unfortunate Fortunatus to accept the challenge from the new presbyter. The date was duly set—August 28, 392.

A large and excited audience turned out for what promised to be good entertainment indeed. "The shorthand reporters opened their notebooks as Augustine threw down the gauntlet," Possidius tells us. His opening challenge was forthright, to say the least! "I now think an error what I had previously thought to be the truth. Whether I am right in my opinion, I desire to hear from you." Suffice it to say the duel was short, succinct, and ended in total victory for Augustine. "The result was that this man, whom everybody had thought so great and learned, was considered to have entirely failed in the defense of his sect. His embarrassment was such that, when soon afterwards he left Hippo, he left it never to return" (*The Life of St. Augustine*, 6).

Turning his attention and expertise across the street to the Donatists, Augustine now challenged them to a similar confrontation. The Donatist bishop, however, knew better than to take on Augustine in a forum in which this former rhetorician was so obviously at home and so outstandingly skillful. He rejected the proposal. Augustine would therefore be compelled to fight the battle on another front.

For a long time, the Donatists had summarized their faith and theological position (to which we shall turn shortly) in slogans, which had in turn been set to music and even become popular songs. Having been cheated of the opportunity to debate formally, Augustine was not above turning his skills and insights to writing a ditty to counter that of the Donatists. The rhythm was popular and the style somewhat vulgar (judged by the standards of a rhetorician). Nevertheless, Augustine was becoming an evangelistic campaigner, and he was willing to employ any method that might champion the cause of his newfound faith.

It is as though this faith of Augustine's knew no bounds. From the Manichees and the Donatists, he now turned his attention to nothing less than the General Council of the church in Africa, which was to meet for the first (and last) time in Hippo in December 393. The council was to be presided over by Aurelius, Bishop of Carthage. In 391, the new primate had written to Augustine, only recently ordained, and from his reply, which we still have available for reference (*Epistolae, 22*), it would seem that these two men (somewhat unevenly yoked) were not only on close terms but also shared similar views about the reforms that were sorely needed in the African church.

Augustine and the African Bishops in Council

THE bishops who attended the council were treated on December 3, 393, to the verbal, theological, and intellectual delights of a newly ordained priest as Augustine stood up before them all and expounded the creed. We know a great deal of what he said to them, for he later set it down and amplified it in a little book entitled *The Faith and the Creed*. The work is essentially an exposition of the creed clause by clause, yet it sets right belief in the context of right living. It was always Augustine's conviction that belief and behavior belong together. After all, his own struggles had not

been purely cerebral. It had been a costly pilgrimage that had at last brought his heart and will into surrender, and he concluded his address to the bishops with words of which his own life was a living testimony:

This is the faith which is handed over to the young Christians, expressed in a few words, which they are to hold faithfully. These few words are made known to believers, that, believing, they may subject themselves to God, being so subject may live righteous lives, living righteously they may cleanse their hearts, and with a pure heart may know what they believe.

—The Faith and the Creed, *10.24*

Augustine's sermon at the council gave him immediate access and exposure to the church in North Africa. Already his friendship with Aurelius, Bishop of Carthage and Primate of Africa since 390, set him at the center of the leaders of the church of his day. He was to hold that position for the rest of his life.

Augustine found a staunch supporter in Aurelius. The primate encouraged him to become the focus of new and brilliant leadership in the church. And Aurelius himself was to be a strong and formative influence in the church, summoning countless councils at Carthage. He also served as another of the father figures to which Augustine had looked all his life. In his letters, Augustine addressed Aurelius as *Auctoritas Tua*—"Your Authority." Aurelius was keen in his turn to support and indeed be a patron to Augustine's monastery, established on the site allotted to it by Valerius in a garden not far from the Christian basilica.

This monastery was to become a significant influence in the church, a seedbed that produced no fewer than ten bishops in the North African church. And we can be certain that all those who left the monastery to serve as such important leaders in the church were tarred with the Augustinian brush! Augustine's friends were to become an army in the orthodox church of the day, reversing its fortunes relative to its opponents—conspicuously the Donatists and the Manichees. Their strategy for renewal and change was classical in shape and in influence. Any who wish to affect the church today would do well to observe carefully the tactics of Augustine and his community of *Servi Dei*—past masters, to a man, in influencing the many by the few and coloring the few from the one.

In any event, for anyone who knew anything of what was happening in the church in North Africa in the last decade of the fourth century, it would have come as no shock to hear that Valerius called for Augustine to serve as Bishop Coadjutor in Hippo. In just a few years as priest, Augustine had come to the forefront of renewal and reinvigoration in the life of the church in Africa. He wrote urgently and somewhat precociously to Valerius, "If Africa should take the lead in stamping out" all the rivals to orthodoxy in her territories, "she ought to be worthy of imitation; but, as far as the greater part of Italy is concerned, and in all or most of the overseas churches, these practices either were never introduced, or, if they sprang up and took root, they were suppressed and destroyed by the vigilant care and censure of holy bishops, who had a true view of the life to come" (*Epistolae, 22.1.4*).

Augustine for Bishop

IT says a great deal for Valerius that he does not appear to have been "threatened" (as contemporary jargon so often puts it) by his new and brilliant young presbyter. On the contrary, there is strong evidence that he already foresaw what a vitally important role Augustine would play in the renewal of the church of his day. In 395 an old and somewhat aloof Valerius wrote secretly to Archbishop Aurelius suggesting that Augustine be consecrated as his bishop coadjutor. Valerius wanted to secure Augustine for Hippo before other vacant bishoprics hijacked him and took him elsewhere.

As we have seen, Aurelius was a friend and admirer of Augustine, so opposition was unlikely to come from that quarter. Not surprisingly, however, there was some opposition to Augustine's election as a bishop. He was, after all, still very young in the faith and in holy orders. Furthermore, now as throughout his life Augustine was not the sort of person people could be indifferent to; there was too much coloring of every kind in him for that. Add to this that it was still regarded in many quarters as rankly unorthodox for a man to be consecrated bishop prior to the death of the existing bishop and you will be able see that the prospect of Augustine's ordination to the episcopate would cause problems in the church of his day.

What exactly was a bishop coadjutor expected to do and to be? There could not be two bishops in a diocese. Such was the argument and the nature of the opposition that initially came from such people as Megalius, Primate of Numidia, who contested against the proposal in the strongest possible language. Indeed, as Possidius tells us, Augustine

A statue of Augustine, bishop's crook in hand, outside the cathedral in Hippo. In his thirty-four years of service as Bishop of Hippo Regius, Augustine radically changed the popular image of the episcopal office in the church of God.

himself initially "refused to receive the episcopate contrary to the practice of the church, while his bishop was still living" (*The Life of St. Augustine*, 8).

However, Valerius still pleaded his case not so much because he wanted Augustine to succeed him at Hippo (so he said in any case) but because of "his bodily weakness and the weight of his years" (*The Life of St. Augustine*, 8). He pleaded that he needed more episcopal help in his diocese. This argument, together with the precedent of the appointment of other bishops coadjutor in some of the other churches overseas, finally carried the day with Augustine and even with Megalius.

There is evidence that Megalius may have had other reasons for opposing Augustine's elevation to the episcopate. At a gathering of bishops, he made a scandalous accusation against Augustine, which Augustine treated with disdain. He was ordered to produce proof of his accusations, and when he could not do so he broke down and presented Augustine with a written exoneration for the calumny, begging his pardon as well as the pardon of his fellow bishops. That episode behind him, Augustine was duly consecrated to the order of bishop in the church of God in 395 at the age of forty-one. He was to spend another thirty-five years ministering in that order.

The following year Valerius died. Augustine succeeded him as Bishop of Hippo Regius, a bishopric which until that point had not enjoyed any particular notoriety. From that time onward, however, it was to enjoy a lasting and worldwide fame. In the thirty-four years Augustine served there as bishop, he was to change radically the popular image of the office of bishop in the church of God by putting his own unique stamp indelibly upon it. The reputation of the Bishop of Hippo was

CHAINED TO THE GOSPEL

to travel through the whole church of his day, both north and south of the Mediterranean. One notable bishop of that time—we know him now as St. Paulinus of Nola—had originally not been a supporter of Augustine, but he was finally given the grace to recognize that Augustine's providential appointment as Bishop of Hippo was "a boon to Christendom."

From the outset, Augustine was determined to renew the episcopal church by renewing expectations concerning the episcopal office, starting with himself and with the church in Hippo. "I do not propose to spend my time in the empty enjoyment of ecclesiastical dignity, but I propose to act as mindful of this—that I must give an account of the sheep committed to me" (*Epistolae*, 22.2.8). And to the congregation at Hippo he said in the sermon he delivered at his episcopal ordination,

May God grant, then, that I may with the help of your prayers, be what you would have me to be— you who wish me well—may be, too, what he would have me be who called me and bade me assume this office. At the same time, whatever I may be, your hope must not be in me. I must speak disparagingly of myself, for I must now speak as your bishop: I want to rejoice in you, not to be inflated by your praise.

Augustine was now the right man in the right place at the right time. The effects of that fortuitous convergence spread throughout the church and the world of his day and are still to be discerned sixteen hundred years later.

CHAPTER SEVEN

CONVICTION AND COMMUNITY

Hippo Regius

LIKE Habakkuk, who was seized by the hair (*Bel and the Dragon,* v. 36), Augustine frequently spoke of himself as a prisoner of the Lord, bound in slavery to the work of a bishop. He was to spend all the rest of his years as Bishop of Hippo, never to leave African soil again, never to venture upon the sea again—no loss so far as he was concerned, for as we have noted, he disliked sea travel intensely.

Based in Hippo, the second port of Africa, he was becoming what one writer calls the Lacordaire of Africa. By the end of his days he would be absurdly revered and renowned—not simply because he was a bishop (there were something between five and seven hundred bishops in the African church by the year 400), but because of the kind of bishop he became. "Among you I am a Christian; for you I am a bishop." It's hard to realize just how extensively Augustine reconstructed the office of bishop in the church of his day. Since the Peace of Constantine (A.D. 313) many bishops had been married men, rich landowners using their position in the church for their own selfish ends. Augustine was by no means an aristocrat of this sort, however. He was still very much the lad from Thagaste; he did not fit into the familiar family groupings and cliques of Hippo or the surrounding countryside of his diocese.

The Traveling Bishop

BY the time Augustine became Bishop of Hippo, the port town had already existed for a thousand years, since before Roman times. Having begun as a Phoenician trading post in the Mediterranean, its streets and houses were laid out in a fashion contrary to the more logical Roman pattern. A journey along the coast of what is today eastern Algeria and Tunisia presents one with a rough coastline of high cliffs and sheer rocks that suddenly give way to the rich, fertile plain of the river Seybouse as one approaches Annaba (Hippo), and the same was true in Augustine's day. At the peak of its Roman period, Hippo was a prosperous and grand city. It looked of course to Carthage as the prime seaport and city of Africa with its population of nearly half a million inhabitants.

Augustine was to spend much of his life as Bishop of Hippo traveling to the many councils of the church, frequently held in Carthage under the enthusiastic leadership of his friend and primate, Aurelius. He undertook these frequent journeys on horseback (never by sea) along the Mejerda Valley, often using the opportunity to travel with fellow bishops from throughout the African church who had formerly been priests in his community. We need to picture him, dressed in the simple black robe, the *birrus,* which as a "Servant of God" he still wore, riding perhaps with Alypius, who had joined him en route to Carthage from his diocesan see at Thagaste. (Incidentally, there is no evidence that Augustine ever went back to Thagaste as bishop either to visit Alypius, who was there now as the bishop, or to see some of his old fellow townsmen. That is a little strange, though perhaps best explained by the more severe weather—especially in the winter—that he would have encountered on the higher ground away from the flat and more temperate seaboard territory of Hippo.) He tells us how he would take advantage of those long hours on horseback on his many journeys to the councils

A plan of the ruins of old Hippo. Excavations begun in 1924 have uncovered much of the Christian quarter, including the main church, a chapel, the bishop's house, and the monastery in a building overlooking the bishop's garden.

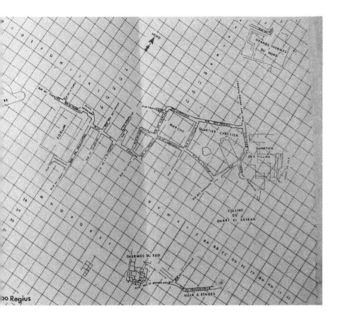

Augustine's Pen

WE must not think that Augustine was an absentee bishop, sitting on committees and boards and consumed by administration. Far from it. It is true, however, that there was a great deal of administration, litigation, and legal arbitration for a bishop to deal with as the spiritual head of his family even as early as the fourth and fifth centuries. In his early days he had requested up to five days a week to study Scripture, uninterrupted by petty administration. That request was rapidly forgotten! He spent many mornings seeking interviews with high government officials, and even more granting such interviews to the senior landowners who sought him out (often before church on Sunday mornings) to ask him to arbitrate for them or give his advice.

He spent many hours on horseback, but that is not the picture that best captures for us the typical Augustine, Bishop of Hippo and spiritual head of the Christian family in his town. As Peter Brown writes, "sitting in the 'secretarium' which adjoined his basilica, so not far from the sacred altar, with a copy of the sacred scriptures close to hand, Augustine thought of himself as a successor of the upright judges of Israel" (*Augustine of Hippo,* p. 196). Such a picture is more typical of his daily work, one of many we need as we seek to build up a collage illustrating his life and daily habits as Bishop in Hippo. ·

The Christian quarter in which Augustine lived can easily be seen today from a nearby hill on which in the nineteenth century a cathedral was built. This cathedral, administered appropriately enough today by Augustinian monks, has on display a portion of Augustine's right arm, the rest of

in Carthage (no fewer than sixty of his recorded sermons were in fact preached at Carthage during such visits) to speak to his friends and fellow travelers "as if to myself."

Frederick van der Meer writes of Augustine that "till the end of his life . . . he continued to move around in Africa; there was no synod that he did not feel compelled to attend, no ecclesiastical committee on which he neglected to be present, no heresiarch whom he did not feel called upon publicly to controvert, and of course time and again he will be asked to go out and preach somewhere on a feast day" (*Augustine the Bishop,* p. 12). He admits that on these journeys he was nearly always asked to preach. "If there was a need for preaching to the people, and I happened to be present, I was hardly ever allowed to keep silent and listen to others, and thus be quick to listen and slow to speech, as James the Apostle enjoins" (*Retractations,* 1, prologue).

his bodily remains being housed at the church of San Pietro Ciel D'oro in Pavia, Italy. Excavations begun in 1924 revealed the fifty acres or so of the original Roman harbor town including the Christian quarter with the main church and adjacent baptistry, a chapel, the bishop's house and library, and the monastery in a building overlooking the bishop's garden. Hard by were the villas of the rich overlooking the harbor.

It was to this harbor that many of Augustine's overseas visitors came bringing letters from notable bishops, such as Paulinus of Nova, and protracted communications from the irritable St. Jerome, that international biblical scholar of his day. And, of course, it was from this harbor that Augustine in his turn dispatched his many letters to overseas dioceses—not least to Rome, the capital of the empire itself.

For Augustine spent his life writing a great many letters—no fewer than two hundred of which are still extant. He employed his pen in controversy not only in writing large volumes of theology during his years as bishop but also in lengthy and at times stern correspondence that was dispatched from the port in Hippo to the far corners of the Mediterranean world. He was to write to such high officials in the Roman Empire as Count Boniface, the military commander in Africa, exhorting him to celibacy and in effect telling him to get his mind on the job at hand! He wrote to Count Marcellinus, the imperial commissioner, suggesting ways in which he should deal with the Donatists. He wrote an informal letter to a young girl, Florentina, who had sought his advice on some perplexing point in her studies. And he often wrote to the smooth and elegant Paulinus, formerly a consul, then a member of a lay community who in the end was consecrated Bishop of Nola.

He had a less fortunate correspondence, to say the least, with the aging biblical scholar St. Jerome of Bethlehem, who was easily offended by any criticism of his scholarship. Shipping letters to and from Bethlehem was at best a somewhat hazardous pursuit. Augustine had written to the prickly old scholar in 394, before his consecration as a bishop and after his first period of extended study of the Scriptures. He disputed some matter of Old Testament translation, basing his arguments on the Greek of the Septuagint version. Jerome, the better biblical scholar of the two, derived his translation from the Hebrew. From that point on their friendship and their correspondence became increasingly troubled.

For his part, Augustine was tactless in the letters he sent to Jerome and careless with the letters he received from him. Jerome, on the other hand, was unduly quick to take offense. From further correspondence, Augustine deduced that Jerome was undermining the veracity of Scripture itself—as biblical scholars are somewhat apt to do. Jerome sought to put this young man in his place: "Do not, because you are young, challenge a veteran in the field of scripture. I have had my time and run my course to the utmost of my strength. It is but fair that I should rest, while you in your turn run" (*Epistolae,* 68.2).

Upon receiving this rebuff Augustine was for the moment ready to make amends, and he drafted a gracious letter of apology. "It remains for me to confess as I now do, my fault as having been the first to offend by writing that letter, which I cannot deny to be mine. . . . I therefore entreat you by the mercy of Christ to forgive me wherein I have injured you" (*Epistolae,* 73.3). Furthermore, he was all too ready to admit the superiority of Jerome's scholarship: "I have not now, and I can never hope to have, such knowledge of the Divine Scriptures as I see you possess" (*Epistolae,* 73.5).

But letters continued to cross until Jerome was driven to distraction. "You are sending me letter upon letter," he complained, "challenging an old man, disturbing the peace of one who asks to be allowed to be silent, and you seem to desire to display your learning" (*Epistolae,* 72.1-2).

This unfortunate dispute went on for years, and for a long time both of these men, equally great in their own fields, were at odds with each other. It took the challenge of Pelagianism to unite them. On this issue Augustine was on safer ground. He had made dogmatic theology his own. So it was that after many years of silence, a letter from Augustine to Jerome on the evils of Pelagianism elicited a generous and complimentary letter from the old scholar in Bethlehem. It proved to be a happy resolution of a somewhat unfortunate and stormy chapter in Augustine's correspondence.

The Rule of St. Augustine

HIPPO was literally Augustine's see—his seat, the place he sat and ministered through his preaching, his teaching, and his writing for over thirty-five years. He was able to carry out this ministry in the name of the gospel because he sought to live primarily in its power and profile. "I speak of that by which alone I live. I distribute that by which I am sustained" (*Sermons,* 10). His way of life spoke eloquently in caring protest against much of the secular and pagan life around him.

Hippo was a wealthy community, not primarily from its seaport industry but from the abundant agriculture on the fertile lands around the plain of the river Seybouse. North Africa was the granary of of the Roman Empire. There was always plenty of food in Hippo. Corn was the principal source of wealth in the region, corn that principally attracted the attention of Roman merchants and Roman taxation authorities. But there was also wine from its famous vineyards and olives from its substantial groves. The latter ensured a plentiful supply of coarse African oil—the midnight oil that Augustine so frequently and economically burned as he labored over his many writings.

At the outset of his ministry in prosperous Hippo, Augustine had none of the advantages of an aristocrat. He was determined to live the simple life of a "Servant of God" in his community of monks—but it is ironically from that position, established and increasingly distinctive as the years went by, that he influenced not only the church in Hippo but the whole community as well as the whole ecclesiastical world beyond the borders of Africa and the Mediterranean. He was never to be an Ambrose, yet in the end he influenced the church more than his former hero. At the beginning of his time in Hippo, the Donatist church was richer and larger than the orthodox church in the community. By the time of his death the situation had been radically reversed. Augustine had established Hippo as a solidly orthodox Christian community and driven out the Donatists. Slowly but surely he came to be known and accepted as the head of the family of Hippo—what he himself so affectionately called *familia Dei.*

Much of Augustine's vision and energy was derived from the cell and community in which he

A portion of the saint's tomb in the church of San Pietro Ciel D'oro depicting Augustine give the Rule—a collection of practical guidelines for community life and personal prayer—to his monastic brethren

had first heard the call to be a Christian. He sought to live the gospel life daily, and it was out of that community life that he was empowered to communicate the gospel. He lived the simple life in community, for which and out of which he wrote his famous Rule of St. Augustine. He wrote the Rule about the year 397, some ten years after his baptism, with a full decade of community life behind him. Shortly after he became bishop, he began to insist that most of his clergy should live with him and share in that community life.

"Among you there can be no question of personal property," he writes, "rather take care that you share everything in common. Your superior should see to it that each person is provided with food and clothing. He does not have to give exactly the same to everyone, for you are not all equally strong, but each person should be given what he personally needs" (*Rule of St. Augustine,* 1.3).

The Rule contains simple and practical guidelines to help in fostering observance of community life and personal prayer. It also contains practical guidelines for the care of the body: "As far as your health allows, keep your bodily appetites in check by fasting and abstinence from food and drink" (*Rule of St. Augustine,* 3.1). He modeled some of his dietary rules on those of his hero Ambrose, exhorting his monks "to fast the whole day" until the main meal "which takes place in the late afternoon." "The sick may have something to eat at any time of the day" and indeed "should obviously receive suitable food" (*Rule of St. Augustine,* 3.2). During meals, passages were to be read from the Scriptures.

On the whole the Rule is not severe. It does not call for many of the privations exercised by monks in Egypt and the East at that time. In Augustine's household the diet was vegetarian, though as Possidius notes, "he sometimes had meat for the sake of his guests or the delicate brethren, and always wine"; and his table service was not entirely austere: "his spoons were silver; the dishes in which the food was served were either earthenware or wood or marble" (*The Life of St. Augustine,* 22).

In the rest of the Rule there are simple guidelines laid down for mutual care and responsibility between the brethren and practical exhortations concerning service and care for others living in community as well as helpful and simple observations concerning the place of authority and obedience. Forgiveness and compassion are set at the very heart of all human relations in the life of the community. In addition to the Rule for men, a Rule for women was also developed, possibly as a guideline for his sister's small community of women, which was run similarly to his own.

It is hard to overestimate the importance of the Rule and the part that these community cells played in helping the church to face life in a world that was coming apart at the seams, a world in which terrorism and lawlessness were perilously on the increase. The cultural and legal influences of the Roman Empire were being slowly eroded beyond recognition by the aggression of hordes of barbarians who soon were to sweep across the Roman world. By the time of Augustine's death, law and order had been swept away along with the culture and manners of the Roman Empire. Indeed, as Augustine lay dying in his bed surrounded by his community in his last days, the barbarian hordes stood at the very gates of Hippo. The communities he helped to establish served to maintain cells of protest in the name of civilization. They were essential in helping to prepare the church for its second major onslaught after its first centuries of persecution—namely, barbarism, social and political disorder, injustice, and disintegration at every level in society.

The Bishop's Household

POSSIDIUS, a member of Augustine's community, recorded many details about his personal life and the life of his community in his biography *The Life of St. Augustine*. "He was always hospitable," Possidius notes, for example. "More-over, what he loved at table was not feasting and drinking but reading and discussion" (22). In the Scriptures there are very few guidelines for the lifestyle of bishops, although among the few are very specific exhortations to all bishops to have "one wife" and to be "given to hospitality" (1 Tim. 3:2; Titus 1:8). Augustine may well have failed rather miserably at the former, but certainly he excelled at the latter. As we have already noted, and as Peter Brown reemphasizes, "Augustine needed the constant response and reassurance of a circle of friends: both to know that he was loved, and to know that there was someone worth loving, encouraged him greatly to love in return" (*Augustine of Hippo,* pp. 200-201).

Alypius was always calling on his friend and presumably staying with the bishop—with Severus, Possidius, Evodius, Profuturus, and all the rest of the household. Once seated at table, Alypius would see the reminder that all visiting friends and bishops were constantly exhorted to observe. To ensure that there would be no malicious gossip at Augustine's table, there was an inscription written in Latin large enough for all to see on his dining table:

Whoever thinks that he is able
To nibble at the life of absent friends
Must know that he is unworthy of this table.

Possidius tells us that "by this he warned all the company to refrain from wanton and damaging anecdotes. And once, when some most intimate friends among his fellow bishops forgot the inscription and broke the rule, he was so upset that he rebuked them sharply, saying that either those lines must be erased from the table or he would get up from the middle of the meal and go to his own room" (*The Life of St. Augustine*, 22).

So in every way, Augustine sought to be as eloquent for the evangelical councils of Christ in the way he lived as in the message he delivered through his preaching and teaching. "His clothes and food, and bedclothes also, were simple and adequate, neither ostentatious nor particularly poor" (*The Life of St. Augustine*, 22). Each year on the anniversary of his ordination, he gave a banquet for the poor. His attitude to almsgiving was pragmatic and unsentimental; he spoke of it always straightforwardly as a matter of transferring capital from this unsafe world to the next.

Altogether the bishop's household was the foundation of his episcopal ministry, providing a haven and an oasis in the midst of a busy life, a vicious society, and a disintegrating world. And that is precisely how the church at its best was to face the end of the empire and the beginning of what history came to know as the Dark Ages.

It is true that as many from his household left to become bishops and as the constituency of the community changed, rendering a community of friends into a monastery of monks and clerics, Augustine felt some sense of loss. A real sense of sadness and bereavement clouded his personal life as the years went by and he became more influential in his public life. He shared this sense of loss in a letter to a friend, warning him that he was likely to encounter something of the same experience as his life and ministry became more intense and fully demanding. He speaks like the father of a large family: "But when you yourself begin to have to surrender some of the very dearest and sweetest of those you have reared, to the needs of churches situated far from you, then you will understand the pangs of longing that stab me on losing the physical presence of friends united to me in the most close and sweet intimacy" (*Epistolae*, 84.1).

The Augustine who on his conversion had sought the quiet life and *otium* of reading, reflection, and prayer was now compelled to enter the fray of public life and find his personal needs being simply forced into the background as life pushed him further and further toward the front of the stage. Eventually he rose to be the highly visible head of a large supporting cast, appearing before larger and larger audiences. The philosopher was becoming increasingly the pastor; the student was becoming increasingly the teacher, a preacher and advocate of the Christian cause against all those who sought to assault orthodoxy. The man of contemplation was finding himself caught up increasingly in local and political as well as ecclesiastical and theological concerns. The promise of retirement was exploding into an active and intensely creative life as a bishop in the church of God.

In two areas of his life Augustine refused to give way to the pressures of administration or the hazards of public life. The first was his heavy schedule of writing (whether letters or theological treatises); the second was his commitment to preaching. Above all he was a man dedicated to words, whether written in his many voluminous books and letters or spoken with powerful rhetoric as the preacher in his cathedral in Hippo and out on the road.

Augustine the Author

BEFORE he became a bishop, Augustine had exercised his pen in writing several books.

Having become a bishop, he by no means departed from such exercise, though the nature of the works he wrote began to change. In the early works he was concerned more with issues of philosophy and culture; during the time of his episcopate his interest turned to a defense of Christian life and faith.

Nearly all of the books Augustine wrote after his ordination are examples of what he would call "occasional theology"—that is, theological writings evoked by a particular occasion, situation, or crisis. As need demanded a statement from the bishop of Hippo, he would be driven not only to preach about it to the growing congregations in his cathedral but also to write about it for a wider audience of scholars, pastors, and theologians throughout the Western world who were increasingly hanging on every word that came from his pen.

Augustine's theology was never that tame and timid variety quietly written in the scholarly leisure of the university or the lecture room. It flowed white hot from the crucible of human history and responded to the challenges and questionings that arose out of crises and contemporary events. He wrote his largest work—*The City of God*—as a response to just such a crisis. It was an attempt to explain and focus some kind of appreciation and understanding of the shattering events of his day in general and in particular to respond to the catastrophic news of the sack of Rome by the Goths in 410. That event sent a wave of shock and fear throughout the Western world; there were widespread suspicions that Christianity was in some way answerable for the drastic shift in international politics. Augustine responded by constructing a whole edifice of theological and metaphysical assertions.

Theology at its best is like the cuckoo, laying its eggs in other birds' nests. In developing his theological insights, Augustine did not hesitate to cross over into other disciplines and sciences. In his many writings, he offers us not merely speculative, academic theology but the cut and thrust of debate, fired at every point by his need to win the day in a contest for orthodoxy, to convince and convert all opponents. Part of our difficulty in approaching Augustine's writings stems from the fact that we come to the battle with one arm tied behind our backs. We find it difficult to perceive the features of the assertions of Augustine's opposite numbers or indeed to be in any way sympathetic to them and all that they represent in their combat with the venerable bishop.

But one of his works has weathered well in varying climates and over many centuries precisely because it is not so much meant to answer an opposing viewpoint as to satisfy a curiosity present in all cultures at all seasons. Augustine's *Confessions,* written around 397, in the early days of his episcopate, is an expression of the warfare Augustine was waging within himself. In some respects it is a sort of spiritual soap opera, laying out in candid detail the many turns he took, for better or worse, in his eventful life.

Augustine felt that he had much that he had to explain about his life prior to his conversion and baptism in order that the world might appreciate the power of God's grace at work in his life. So he wrote a record of his own experience of the work of grace—amazing grace—a story that gives a flesh-and-blood reality to much of his later theology. It is a book in which he recalls and records the Scriptures on every page—those same Scriptures that were so lucidly expounded for him by Bishop Ambrose and to which he in turn as a bishop devoted his whole life of preaching and teaching. It is a book of passion and color; it is tortuous and intense: it is all of these things because Augustine is all of these things himself in ways that only he can get in touch with through the written record.

Augustine was not merely a hard-working author but a compulsive writer. Throughout his entire life he worked late into the night on his letters and his books, and toward the end of his life he went further still, reviewing all that he had previously written, adapting, correcting, and reviewing all of the material down to the last jot and tittle!

Augustine the Preacher

BUT as we have noted, Augustine was a man of the spoken word as well as the written word, known for his eminence as a preacher and teacher in the African church. All his years of training in rhetoric had led him to become a rhetorician for Christ, and he saw his calling to be a bishop above all else as the calling to be an apostolic, preaching man. In the opinion of Frederick van der Meer,

Through his genius for the right word he surpasses all the Church Fathers. Never once does he fail to make an idea unforgettable. Never once does he fail, when he desires to do so, to turn a simple statement into an aphorism. He never uses the sharpness of his mind to wound; on the contrary, every word he says carries its conviction by reason of an irresistible tenderness. Everyone who reads a number of his sermons will carry away the same impression as the men of his day, for no words from the pulpit have ever so fully come from the heart or

combined that quality with such brilliance as did the words spoken by this one man in this remote corner of Africa.

—Augustine the Bishop, *p. 412*

Of course the setting of a crowded church where members of the congregation took down the sermons (or, as his contemporary biographer Possidius tells us, "brought shorthand writers with them") afforded a stage, an environment, and an atmosphere to which Augustine, the former rhetorician, would rapidly and readily respond. In fact, Augustine had a weak voice.

"We beg you for silence," he once began by telling the large congregation when he was preaching, as he frequently did, for his friend Archbishop Aurelius in Carthage. "Then, after the strain which was put upon it yesterday, our voice may last out for at least a short while." He knew how to get the crowd on his side and to coax them to full attention!

"Yesterday, the crowd stood packed together into the uttermost corners and people were not very quiet, which made it difficult for our voice, for that voice is not strong enough to be heard by everybody unless there is absolute silence."

Possidius believed that Augustine was at his most compelling in the setting of the church and the liturgy, that his power there exceeded that in his considerably powerful written words: "No one can read what he wrote on theology without profit. But I think that those were able to profit still more who could hear him speak in church and see him with their own eyes" (*The Life of St. Augustine*, 31).

It is in the fourth volume of his book on Christian doctrine that Augustine shares with us his passion for preaching and teaching. In this section of the book, which he added in 426, just four years before his death, he reflects upon a ministry of thirty-five years of preaching and teaching the Christian gospel. From this source and also from many of his sermons and writings, the student of Augustine can glean some wonderful guidelines for the art and craft of preaching.

From the outset, says Augustine, the preacher must approach his calling with awe and a sense of the transcendent. Information is not enough; at some point it must give place to inspiration and proclamation. "The sound of our words strike the ear, but the master is within. You must not think that any one learns from a man. The noise of our voice can be no more than a prompting; if there is no teacher within, that noise of ours is useless. . . . Outward teachings are but a kind of helps and promptings: the teacher of hearts has his chair [*cathedra*] in heaven" (*Treatise on St. John's Gospel,* 1.264). For the salvation of the preacher is itself tied up with the salvation of his people. Preacher and people wear the same pilgrim shoes: "Why do I preach? Why do I sit here upon the cathedra? What do I live for? For this one thing alone, that we may one day live with Christ! This is my endeavor, my honor, my fame, this is my joy and my treasured possession! And if you have not heard me attentively, and I have for all that not remained silent, then I have at least saved my own self, but I do not desire to attain everlasting salvation without you" (*Sermons,* 17.2).

Peter Brown says, "This is the secret of Augustine's enormous power as a preacher. He will make it his first concern to place himself in the midst of his congregation; to appeal to their feelings for him, to react with immense sensitivity to their emotions, and so, as the sermon progressed to

sweep them up into his own way of thinking" (*Augustine of Hippo,* p. 251). It is the cry of St. Paul, that other great man of the Word, in another key: "Woe to me if I do not preach the gospel" (1 Cor. 9:16). Or, as Augustine summarized it, "You stand in a safer place in hearing, than we in preaching" (*Sermons,* 197.7).

Augustine was under no delusions about the resource material available to the preacher: it was, it is, and it always will be the Word of God, revealed to us through the words of Scripture. We should not be surprised, therefore, that most of his preaching arises directly out of the lectionary and liturgy of the day. "The Holy gospel which we heard just now as it was being read, has admonished touching the remission of sins. And on this subject, must you be admonished now by my discourse. For we are ministers of the word—not our own word, but the Word of our God and Lord" (*Sermons,* 114.1).

Of course, he came to his calling as a preacher straight from his training and craft as a rhetorician in the ornate and somewhat flowery style that was characteristic of Late Antiquity. Much of this style was derived from the heyday of classical oratory— the days of such masters as Cicero. As we read Augustine's sermons we are certainly aware that the bishop is still speaking very much as a rhetorician, but we are also aware of genuine spontaneity and a willingness to depart from style for its own sake in order to take the words given to him by the Lord: "I shall tell you what the Lord made vouchsafe to me," he confidently tells his congregation. Style was for Augustine after his baptism secondary to the overriding need to make the content clear and to communicate the gospel at all costs. "What matters it to us, what the grammarians please to rule? It were better for us to be guilty of a barbarism so that you understand, than that in our propriety of speech you are left unprovided" (*On the Psalms,* 36.3.6). Augustine the aesthete was well and truly superseded after his ordination by Augustine the preacher with a passion for souls. "Preach wherever you can, to whom you can and as you can" (*Sermons,* 19.2).

Of course expectations concerning the preacher in that day were very different from expectations concerning bishops today, but it was also very much the case that the behavior of the congregation in Augustine's basilica was very different from the behavior of the average cathedral congregation in our own times. In Augustine's day they would applaud if the preacher pleased them, interrupt if the preacher confused them, and shout out and heckle if they found themselves in disagreement with the preacher. Preaching in Augustine's time could not be mistaken for a lecture or a monologue. "I see that you anticipate me by your crying out," he said at one point. "So you know what I am about to say, you anticipate it by your crying out" (*On the Psalms,* 88.1.10). In many ways, then, the sermons Augustine offered in the Cathedral of Peace (ironically that was the name it received at its dedication) would be considered out of the ordinary by most modern preachers; every one of them was in effect a dialogue sermon.

Augustine would typically seek to restrain his congregation from easy applause and uncommitted responses. On one occasion, when he was lambasting theater attendance (as he so frequently did), the congregation applauded his remarks in spite of the fact that many of them regularly attended the local theater when their somewhat overbearing bishop was not looking in their direction!

Augustine turned their spontaneous enthusiasm against them with an accusation: "What I want is good conduct," he told them. "Let your praise of wisdom be in the manner of your lives and express it not through noise [applause] but through harmony with the law of God" (*Sermons,* 311.4).

Augustine would not have condemned the practice of powerful evangelistic preaching today. He would have turned it to advantage—away from merely being a spiritual massage and toward an active recruitment for disciplined discipleship. "It is easy to hear Christ, easy to praise the gospel, easy to applaud the preacher: but to endure unto the end is peculiar to the sheep who hear the Shepherd's voice" (*On St. John's Gospel,* 45.13).

Persuasion is of the essence in preaching. Augustine unapologetically borrowed from his former hero Cicero when he wrote "to teach is a necessity, to please is a sweetness, to persuade is a victory." He added that "the eloquence of the discourse pleases in vain unless that which is learned is implemented in action. It is necessary, therefore, for the ecclesiastical orator, when he urges that something be done, not only to teach that he may instruct, and to please that he may hold attention, but also to persuade that he may be victorious" (*Epistolae,* 21.5).

So Augustine the preacher held the sermon to be an event—"One loving heart sets another on fire." The astute preacher will always be on the lookout for signs of weariness in the congregation, he tells us, and will respond "with discreet cheerfulness, and suited to the matter at hand, or something very wonderful and amusing, or, it may be something painful and mournful" (*De Cat. Rud.,* 13.19.209). But he was under no illusions about the problems and handicaps of a polished, prepared script. How can the preacher really be responsive to the congregation and fulfill the purposes of preaching unless there is an element of spontaneity and freshness in his preaching? A preacher cannot be buried in a manuscript—never mind how well-manicured the words or how carefully prepared the prose. "Of what use is a gold key if it will not open what we wish?" Above all the preacher must reach out with analogy, metaphor, and illustration to touch his congregation and appeal to what they already know and experience in order that they may be taken beyond their present knowledge and experience.

So in a sense the preacher must be what Augustine was—a poet, a wordsmith, and most importantly someone whose mind is perpetually open to images, for it is in this area that we find the true genius of Augustine's preaching. "It is in and through symbols," writes Thomas Carlyle in *Sartor Resartus*, "that man, consciously or unconsciously, lives, works and has his being: those ages, moreover, are accounted the noblest which can the best recognize symbolic word and prize it the highest. For is not a symbol ever, to him who has eyes for it, some dimmer or clearer revelation of the godlike. Of this thing, however, be certain: wouldst thou plant for eternity, then plant into the deep infinite faculties of man, his fantasy and his heart."

Augustine knew instinctively that he was in the business of planting for eternity, and he knew, therefore, that his preaching must plant seeds of God's word in the imagination and in the heart of the congregation. So it was that he viewed the task of a preacher as rooted in the need for images and allegories that could make the sermon resonate with the subconscious experiences and knowledge of his congregation. There can be no great preach-

ing without this kind of realization. As Peter Brown suggests, for Augustine

the need for such a language of "signs" was the result of a specific dislocation of the human consciousness. In this, Augustine takes up a position analagous to that of Freud. In dreams also, a powerful and direct message is deliberately diffracted by some psychic mechanism, into a multiplicity of "signs" quite as intricate and absurd, yet just as capable of interpretation, as the "absurd" or "obscure" passages in the Bible. Both men, therefore, assume that the proliferation of images is due to some precise event, to the development of some geological fault across a hitherto undivided consciousness: for Freud, it is the creation of an unconscious by repression; for Augustine, it is the outcome of the Fall. For the Fall has been among many other things a fall from direct knowledge into indirect knowledge through signs. The "inner fountain" of awareness dried up. Adam and Eve found that they could only communicate with one another by the clumsy artifice of language and gestures.

—Augustine of Hippo, p. 251

Brown is right on target with this assessment. Every advertiser and television evangelist knows what Augustine knew and what Freud knew. It is rather sad that so often the clergy of the established churches seem to have forgotten all this—or preferred never to know it.

In any event, we find rich stores of analogy, image, verbal gestures, and metaphors in all of Augustine's sermons. Who could ever forget his words about the avarice and acquisitiveness of the rich: "You believe that they are satisfied? Far from it! They no longer desire to drink from a beaker

Monica and Augustine featured on a stained glass window in the church of San Pietro Ciel D'oro in Hippo. We do better to put saints on windows than on pedestals, for we are not meant to focus on them but to see through them—to God who stands beyond.

because they thirst after the whole river!" (*Sermons*, 50.6). Or again, "What is so uncertain as a rolling thing?" he asks his congregation. "Is it not fitting that money itself is stamped round, because it remains not still?" (*On the Psalms*, 83.3).

On Sunday mornings, most days of the week, and whenever the bishop was in town, the Christians at Hippo could expect preaching more powerful than anything they could find in the rival church of the Donatists across the street, of the Manichees up the road, or indeed in the large theater in town. And so it was for almost forty years. Augustine the bishop was also Augustine the judge and pastor and prolific writer of theology, but above all Augustine the powerful preacher and advocate of the orthodox Christian cause. The impact of his words of advice, counsel, or exhortation reverberated around Africa and indeed the Mediterranean world of his day and have continued to do so for sixteen hundred years since.

Let us allow Peter Brown to complete our picture of Augustine as the preacher and etch it into our imagination.

Augustine would not even have been physically isolated from his audience, as a modern preacher would be, who stands in a pulpit above a seated congregation. The congregation of Hippo stood throughout the sermon, while Augustine usually sat in his cathedra. The first row therefore would have met their bishop at eye level, at only some five yard's distance. Augustine would have spoken directly to them, quite extemporary . . . but there could be little room in Augustine's approach for the relaxed mood of the contemplative. An audience would identify itself only with an excited man: and Augustine would be excited for them; vehement yearnings for peace, fear, and guilt—these are the emotions to which Augustine's audience reacted with shouts and groans.

—Augustine of Hippo, *p. 251*

CHAPTER EIGHT

CONTROVERSY AND COMBAT

Augustine the Theological Crusader

WE now come to the stage where we can no longer evade a side of Augustine's life and work that is doubtless the most unacceptable to the twentieth-century outlook. It is difficult to live with Augustine of Hippo for very long and not be repelled by his aggression and his apparent love of controversy. In an age that sets opinions above truth and at least ostensibly champions freedom in belief and religion, Augustine's ruthless assertion of truth over error appears tyrannical and narrow-minded—serious and damning accusations in any event, but especially when they are directed against a Christian preacher and bishop. Before we enter the jungle of Augustine's various controversial engagements, we need some kind of map, some points of reference in order to avoid wandering into inappropriate judgments, for in these regions it is never long before it becomes difficult to see the forest of common sense for the theological trees.

We need to clarify two basic points concerning Augustine of Hippo before we enter the fray. The first is that saint he may well be (indeed, the church reminds us that this is the case at least once each year, on August 28), but hero most certainly he is not, as his actions in the midst of combat and controversy make clear. Our contemporary world is not free of heroes—no age has ever been—but we've seen through most of them, be they political, sports, or religious figures, and we are somewhat disillusioned. It is neither easy nor painless to see their feet of clay.

But thank God saints are not heroes. Hagiography—the study of holiness—is largely a lost art today. For the truth is that you are supposed to be able to see through the saints—right through them—which is probably why we do better to put them in stained glass windows than on pedestals. (Pedestals are for heroes; they offer somewhat precarious footing.) "A saint is someone who lived a long time ago, who has never been adequately researched." Such may well be our contemporary definition of a saint, the implication being that adequate research would uncover flaws, faults, and failings. We certainly can't afford to look at our heroes too closely.

Yet in the Western church, the definition of a saint stands twentieth-century values on their head and turns all the arguments back to front and inside out. For the church in fact defines a saint as someone who has been so hollowed out (generally by suffering) and rendered so transparent that God could work at least three miracles right through them! The saints are not a race of good men and women who appear to improve through their religious observances. They tend instead to be bad men and women who by grace are made holy. There is all the difference in the world between the two—and we should not confuse them.

By the world's standards, Alypius would seem a good deal more saintly than Augustine, and indeed he became a bishop before Augustine did. But the church does not honor him with beatification, and history has largely forgotten him except as a friend of Augustine. Augustine was not a self-made man; he was a weak man whom grace (that random factor in the chemistry of creation) made strong. He was not a nice man; at times he was a bad man and frequently a rather sad man, whom grace—again, *grace*—made holy and blessed. The first of the beatitudes in modern translation affords us a fair summary of Augustine's life: "Blessed are those who know their need of God."

So the vanity, the histrionics, the hypochondria—all were there in Augustine to the last moment of his life on earth. Grace does not annihilate nature; it slowly perfects it. It is not particularly important that much of what Augustine brought into the life of the church and into his discipleship and ministry were all there before. He brought his ambition from his days as a rhetorician to win debates on behalf of the church, and when he won he believed that the debate was the Lord's—and who is to say that he was mistaken? In his earlier life he flattered emperors who claimed divine attributes, and he did so with eloquence. Later he praised the living God and the divinity of Christ with equal if not surpassing eloquence. There is still the same blood in his veins and the same adrenalin in his system: it did not depart at his conversion but was rather harnessed afresh and dedicated to a new cause. His worship of heroes and father figures in the days of his unbelief was transposed into a new loyalty to a heavenly Father "whose service is perfect freedom."

In all things, Augustine brought to his Christian combat all the tricks of the old trade, rededicating them to the service of a new faith. We must not, therefore, be too shocked to find little that we would want to praise as open-minded, broadminded, or open-ended. Rhetoric of that sort did not win the day in the ancient empire of Rome, nor would such rhetoric have won the day for the Christian cause in the vicious and competitive climate of the Late Antiquity or the early Middle Ages. Does it really fare any better today? If truth is what in the end will set us free, it will need stern advocates who are as willing to take arms against spiritual and mental slavery as they have ever been

to remove slavery in any of its other forms. Orthodox Christians believed the church had found such an advocate in the dark days of the fifth century. We might want to ask where such advocates are to be found at the close of the twentieth century.

The second point of reference we need as we seek to find our way through the jungle of Augustine's controversies is more difficult to discern. As we cut our way through the theological undergrowth, we shall be asking ourselves again and again how on earth the church could permit the simple gospel of Jesus of Nazareth to become so caught up in all the wrangling that took place. Wasn't most of it just so much splitting of hairs, so much needless debate over how many angels can dance on the head of a pin? Was there really no theological middle ground that could have accommodated both Pelagius and Augustine peacefully?

There are at least two answers to these popular and persuasive questions. Theology in the twentieth century, far from being "the queen of the sciences," no longer occupies any place in popular enthusiasm. If we truly want to identify with the theological struggles of the fourth and fifth centuries, we need to transpose those themes into new keys and orchestrate them for very different instruments. Perhaps it is the new mythology of science fiction that more than anything else today preaches at us with an eloquence sufficient to capture our imagination and fuel our dreams and our hopes. Metaphysics may have disappeared in the form we knew it from the marketplace only to reappear in new forms from new directions in productions that have made their way into the movie theaters and onto our television screens.

A Man for Our Season?

To understand Augustine, we need to understand the dilemma of the church in any age as it seeks to proclaim a full and balanced gospel. Truth is necessarily larger than our finite apprehension of it and more rounded than our somewhat flat perspectives on it. The church has traditionally presented its creeds in deliberately paradoxical and apparently self-contradictory formulas: Jesus is God and he is man; our one God is triune, three in one and one in three. Difficult though that all inevitably is, the problem is further compounded by our approach at any given time to these paradoxes. We do not come to them from neutral territory; the dice are always heavily loaded before we start. All individuals, as all ages, begin from a position that is already prejudiced, taking some bit of the truth for granted and reaching out for the rest of it. Nor can we ameliorate our biases by adding to them purely balanced and objective statements, try though we might. Indeed, the record of Christian doctrine throughout Christian history should perhaps be entitled "In Praise of Heresy"! For truth to tell, the orthodoxy of one age may well emerge as the heresy of the next. The hero of faith in one era is likely enough to lead others who start from a different bias in another era into blatant heresy.

As he went into combat, Augustine was not intent on supplying balanced and objective statements for balanced objective people living in a balanced and objective age! He was deeply involved in dialectic. In a different age, who knows? Pelagius might have been the man of orthodoxy and Augustine branded as the man of heresy.

There are few men or women who are orthodox saints for all seasons.

Yet, as a controversialist and a man of theological combat, surely Augustine is a man for our season almost as much as he was for his own. For we, like him, are perched precariously on the edge of a precipice. He found cause for optimism in the past; there was little to warrant it in his present or the future. We, too, face a most uncertain future, despite the fact that popular opinion, unmindful of the warnings from secular prophets, authors, and artists alike, looks away, as blind to its dire prospects as were the Gadarene swine. Popular opinion finds the warnings of an Augustine somewhat morbid and unduly pessimistic about human nature. Yet the hyperbole he used as a prophetic corrective is exactly what is needed in our time—even if most of the time it is not wanted.

As our civilization approaches the second millennium, we have plenty of counterparts to the Pelagians among our politicians, popular media prophets, and assorted secular high priests who find talk of the Fall and mankind's desperate plight too morbid by half. We need some voice beyond that of our artists, writers (not least our science fiction writers), and psychologists to reassert the half of the truth that is less pleasant to hear. Sadly, in a world where there is already fierce competition for the attention of the public, such voices will not be heard any more than they were in Augustine's day without amplification. We must not expect Augustine as we enter these combats with him to be a dispassionate, donnish delight: he is (because he has to be) the aggressive, passionate pastor, scarred with the wounds of the battle, yet single-minded and well provisioned for the crusade.

The Origins of Donatism

WHEN Augustine became bishop of Hippo in 396, succeeding the late Bishop Valerius, he was beginning little less than a lifetime's crusade. As we have already noted, there was in the very same block as Augustine's cathedral church— the *basilica Pacis*—a larger, more impressive cathedral church housing another bishop with a larger congregation: the church of the Donatist sect. While Augustine was preaching and leading his people in worship, he was able to hear music coming from this other place of worship—music that he in typically exaggerated style calls the "roaring of lions." Especially in the early years of his episcopate, Augustine was to express himself passionately in opposition to the Donatist sect. We need to know who they were and why Augustine should almost single-handedly have taken them on in open combat.

The sect originated in the years immediately following the vicious persecution of the Christians by the emperor Diocletian. For the greater part of the reign of Diocletian, the Christian church enjoyed comparative tranquility. But on February 23, 303, violent persecution broke out on a grand scale as Diocletian ordered the burning of Christian churches and especially the burning of all Christian books and copies of the Scriptures. At the outset the persecution was directed principally against the clergy as the custodians of the church and stewards of the mysteries of the Christian faith in the written word of the Scriptures. A further edict, however, issued the following year, extended the persecution to the laity also. This persecution was to last, in varying intensity from place to place and time to time, until the Peace of Constantine A.D. 313, when Christianity finally became an official religion in the Roman Empire.

During the period of persecution, countless Christian clergy and laity remained faithful even to death, refusing to hand over Christian Scriptures to the Roman authorities. But there was also a large number who renounced their faith in the face of torture. Among these there were bishops as well as priests—especially in Numidia—who handed over Christian books and copies of the Scriptures, failing to stand firm in the moment of trial.

Little wonder, therefore, that when the Peace of Constantine came and the persecution ceased there was much bitterness that divided whole families and congregations. It was not unlike France after the Second World War, when many communities were torn apart by resentment for those who had collaborated with the enemy rather than standing firm. It took much love and forebearance to accept such people back into community life when so many still felt the pain of the loss of those who had fallen in combat.

So it was after the Peace of Constantine. Many clergy and some laity were branded as *traditores*—traitors. They had literally "handed over" *(traditores)* copies of the Scriptures to the enemy. In the eyes of many, this capitulation constituted a betrayal of Christ, a sin so serious that they ought not to be allowed back into the communion and fellowship of the church unless they were rebaptized. Donatus led a group of those who maintained that clergy who had capitulated during the Diocletianic persecution had thereby rendered themselves invalid as ministers of the Word and that they could no longer validly celebrate the sacraments. Donatus was eventually made bishop in Carthage and politically supported by groups at court both in Rome and Milan. The Donatists proceeded to grow in numbers, influence, and power in the empire.

Confrontation and Debate in Carthage

THE Donatists appealed to a council in Rome and were denounced. A specially convened council at Arles clearly and resolutely declared that the spiritual standing of the one who ministered the sacraments does not in any way render the sacrament valid or invalid: it is, thank God, an objective gift that is not hindered by human frailty or sinfulness.

Yet the fire of Donatism spread rapidly, especially in the church of North Africa and in the province of Numidia. It was right on Augustine's doorstep. Soon it became a political as well as a religious issue. Donatists were in effect both religious and political zealots, their zeal and clearly defined objectives firing something deep within the African mentality. Later their political and religious zeal fueled terrorism.

An extreme party within the Donatist movement, who came to be known as the *Circumcellions* (literally, "those who live around the tents"), took to roaming the countryside in bands, engaging in arson and pillaging, not least among the farms of Christians located in far-flung areas, but soon enough in the towns and cities also. They seized Bishop Maximianus of Bagai, desecrated his cathedral while he watched, stabbed him, and threw him off the church tower. Strangely, and no

doubt miraculously, the bishop was not killed by the fall; a convenient dung heap nearby softened his fall and saved his life! Augustine's biographer Possidius also suffered at the hands of the Donatist terrorists. They burned his home, captured him, and beat him. And we are told that on one of his many journeys Augustine himself "accidentally" took the wrong road, which saved him from an ambush (and almost certain death) at the hands of the tent people.

It was not long before Augustine took up the theological cudgels against the Donatists. They were in the majority in most African cities, and right on the doorstep of Augustine's own church claiming to be the only pure and holy church in Hippo.

Religious Fanaticism

WHEN Circumcellions seized a church building they would literally seek to "purify" it, typically by scraping down the walls, washing and scrubbing the floors, destroying the altars, and pouring salt into the ground on the sites where "profane" and "sacrilegious" altars had previously stood. From the point of view of Donatism, those in the established church had allied themselves with the *traditores* and so had polluted the church of Jesus Christ. The Donatists believed that the church, like the ark of Noah, should be well-tarred both inside and outside, that it should keep within itself the good waters of baptism and should keep out the defiling waters of the world. They regarded the established church as the church of Judas. Now that Christianity had become popular and easy to profess, the Donatists were seeking the ideal of the pure and the holy church. Some people might be surprised that Augustine did not go along with this sharply defined and powerfully witnessing church. If he were really the zealot and puritan that history has so often suggested he was, there should have been much in the Donatist cause that would have appealed to him. As it stands, however, two things in Augustine's personal life drew him back from the edges of Donatism and made him the theological champion of the established church.

In the first place, Augustine came to the whole controversy with the benefit of a larger view of the church than was afforded by the limited horizons of the African church. His formative years as a Christian were spent "overseas" in Milan, Rome, and Italy. This gave him a broader perspective on the church and its place in the world at large. There was something claustrophobic and ingrown about the African church. Its internal ecclesiastical squabbles were colored with other divisions of tribe, language, and geography. Religious wars are never purely religious. They represent the convergence of many motivations, of which nationalism and tribalism are generally the most powerful. Augustine had traveled enough to get his eyes above the African skyline and to see the church in relation to its worldwide mission, accepting within its walls the good, the bad, and the indifferent.

But there was a more fundamental attitude in Augustine's makeup that took him right to the heart of the issue at hand. In Augustine the convert the Donatists found their most articulate and unrelentless critic. Their attitudes struck at something very deep within Augustine's life. There was in much of Donatism a tendency to revert to the law. In their search for purity, the Donatists had slid into legalism and rigorism. In Augustine's book, there are two overriding factors to which all desires for purity and legalism must finally give way. First, there is the overriding will of God: "Who shall remove the preordained course of God?" he was to demand (*On the Psalms*, 32.14). Or on a more sarcastic note he would chide the Donatists with these words: "The clouds roll with thunder, that the house of the Lord shall be built throughout the earth: and these frogs sit in their marsh and croak—we are the only Christians!" (*On the Psalms*, 95.11).

There is much both of Job and Paul in Augustine's theology at this point. It was God's will and providence that he should give his son to the world and the sacraments to the church. How could the unworthiness of any minister of those sacraments hinder these great gifts from God? "The spiritual value of the sacraments," Augustine tells us, "is like light: although it passes among the impure it is not polluted."

Right Faith and Wrong Actions

YET for Augustine the issue went even further. In his own pilgrimage, it had been by grace and grace alone that he had been saved. Grace was the free gift of Jesus Christ; it was certainly no purity within Augustine that had saved the day for him. How could a minister ever hope to approach the altar to celebrate the sacred mysteries if he had to rely upon his own worthiness? He must rely upon the free gift of Christ. All ministers, *traditores* or not, are in effect traitors—for all have sinned and fallen short of the glory of God. The test of the true church is not whether it makes good men perfect but whether it makes bad men holy—and that holiness is always the work of grace and grace alone, appropriated in one baptism.

Augustine rejected the notion that the church was to be a sect organized around consistent moral behavior. We are justified not by right actions but by right beliefs. Here Augustine built a solid bridge between the church of St. Paul and the church that at the Reformation was to reaffirm justification by faith as opposed to justification by works. The *traditores* were sinners like anyone else, and baptism was for them, as for all, the medicine prescribed precisely for such sickness.

Each age tends to point to some one special sin or failing that it assumes to be *the capital sin* that puts the sinner beyond the pale of baptism. It is interesting to surmise what that sin might be in the midst of the secular moralism of our day, but whatever it is, it is the task of the church to refuse today as in every age to circumscribe the powers of the medicine of baptism, for that is the universal sacrament prescribed by a merciful Physician to heal the souls of men and women—whatever their sins may be.

"While the Donatist view of the church had a certain rock-like consistency," writes Augustinian scholar Peter Brown, "Augustine's church was like an atomic particle: it was made up of moving elements, a field of dynamic tensions, always threatening to explode" (*Augustine of Hippo,* p. 223). Such is the power of God's will and God's love given freely to his church.

Augustine could sniff even the edges of sectarianism and elitism; his vision of the church of God was not that it was to create a little "kingdom of saints" snuggling up to their bishop for warmth and protection from an alien world. That had not been the mantle that Ambrose had handed over to him. The church had indeed reached a fork in the road: was it to go the way of Ambrose or the way of Cyprian of Carthage (a bishop of the established church who was nonetheless somewhat small-minded and small-hearted), to whom many Donatists turned for support and advocacy for their cause.

Augustine spent many of the early years of his episcopate in debate and combat with the Donatists, steadily winning ground over the years. Yet it was the emperor Honorius who brought the matter to a head on August 25, 410, when he summoned the bishops of both churches to a conference. At last there was to be what Augustine had wanted for so long—a public confrontation. The conference, or *collatio* ("comparison"), as it was to be called, exploded into being on May 18, 411, when some 284 Donatist bishops from all over Africa assembled in the city of Carthage. The meeting was to be chaired by Flavius Marcellinus, a devout and scrupulously conscientious representative of the established church.

The scene and dynamics of the great confrontation were exactly the sort in which Augustine would be most at home. He had acquired considerable experience in the tactics of public debate in the very early years after his ordination, when he had equipped himself in confrontation with the Manichees. He had ridden home to victory then; he would do so again on the larger stage and for the more important cause of Christian orthodoxy versus Donatism.

Victor in Debate

THE conference lasted just three sessions, on the first, third, and eighth of June 411. For the first two sessions Augustine held his fire while Petilian of Cirta, representing the Donatist forces, manipulated the fair-minded chairman and drove the orthodox forces (who were largely in disarray) back into their corner. Augustine's colleagues Alypius and Possidius were vocal, but they unloaded their fire far too quickly and with little sense of direction. Possidius lost his temper and was rude, while Alypius failed to employ any effective debating tactics. He could not resist using the occasion to tell everyone how wonderfully well everything was going in his little diocese at Thagaste, where apparently peaceful unity reigned under his outstanding leadership!

At the final session, Augustine stepped forward. He had the brief for the orthodox case at his fingertips like a well-mannered barrister, confident of carrying the case and winning the day. He answered point by point (apparently impromptu) the carefully prepared manifesto of the Donatist case that Petilian had prepared and presented so brilliantly in the previous sessions.

In the early morning of June 9, Marcellinus delivered judgment: the Donatists had no case. "Let falsehood once detected bow its neck to the truth made manifest."

Coercion by the State

IN the years that followed, the state took over the larger share of work in repressing the Donatists, employing legal coercion to force them into the orthodox fold. As we might expect, they resisted such efforts; in fact, many of the more extremist of their flock, especially of the Circumcellions, preferred suicide to submission. Some of their bishops and leaders made gallant and honorable stands against the laws of persecution enforced upon them by the state. In 420, Gaudentius, bishop of the huge Donatist church at Timgad, went to his magnificent basilica when the imperial officials were approaching the city to enforce the laws against the Donatist church. He threatened to burn himself and his congregation in the basilica rather than submit.

In all it was a sad and ugly conflict. Augustine had no stomach for the kind of political combat that emerged after the conference in Carthage. The army was brought in to enforce the law. There was much bloodshed, and all in the name of the true Christian faith. Soon enough the arguments were refined to the point that there was no possibility for any middle ground, no room left for compromise or compassion. Even the fair-minded Marcellinus, who had so carefully and wisely chaired the conference (he was a sort of earlier version of Thomas More), fell afoul of the imperial authorities. He was arrested on September 13, 413, taken to a public park, and beheaded at dawn.

Matters slipped out of the hands of the church as the empire took over fighting for the cause of orthodoxy. It is one of those chapters in the history of the church of which we can be least proud. It should stand always as a reminder of what happens when Christians seek to build their empire upon the foundations of the kingdoms of this world, of what happens whenever we seek to legislate morality.

Bullies love to fight for a "righteous" cause, to secure spiritual ends with weapons drawn from their worldly arsenal. Although Augustine had been successful in championing the cause of orthodoxy at the conference in Carthage, the ensuing bloodshed (not least the murder of Marcellinus) drove him back to Hippo, where he resolved never to return to Carthage for any length of time. The established church was in danger of winning the battle but losing the day. Augustine made a written appeal to the Donatists in a long and careful work that appeared in 412. He appealed to a certain *largesse du coeur* in his readers, orthodox and Donatist alike, for clearly the suppression of Donatism by the imperial and secular authorities was not going to work.

> *We know how many of you—and perhaps all, or almost all,—are accustomed to say: "Oh, if they could only come together! If they could only have a discussion sometime and the truth emerge from their debate!" Well, it happened, falsehood was found guilty and truth revealed. Why then is unity still shunned and charity scorned? . . . The error which separated us has already been vanquished in the meetings with your bishops. May the time come when the devil in your hearts may be vanquished and Christ be favorable to his·flock, gathered in peace as he commanded.*

For Augustine it had been a sort of Pyrrhic victory; he could not wait to get back to Hippo, his library, and his writing. "I have resolved," he says with a note of weariness in his voice, "to devote my time entirely, if the Lord will, to the labor of studies pertaining to ecclesiastical writing: in doing which I think that I may, if it please the mercy of God, be of some service even to future generations" (*Epistolae,* 151.13).

Having been saddened by the outcome at the conference, Augustine returned to Hippo to face matters of even greater urgency, matters that would have ramifications more far-reaching than mere ecclesiastical squabbles. The very foundations of the empire—the empire to which the church had appealed against the Donatists, the empire that had agreed to champion the church's cause—were crumbling. The writing was clearly on the wall. Indeed, on August 24, 410, the walls of Rome itself had fallen to the onslaughts of a barbarian invasion. Alaric the Goth led his men into the sack of the eternal city—the heart of empire, law, order, and justice. It felt like the end of the world.

Jerome and Augustine, right, an oil painting in the church of San Pietro in Ciel D'oro

CHAPTER NINE

A Tale of
Two Cities

The Sack of Rome: A.D. 410

IF erosion in the structures of empire, law, and order were dimly in evidence by the close of the fourth century, they had hit the headlines at the outset of the fifth century. St. Jerome, that somewhat pusillanimous biblical scholar from Bethlehem, wrote to console his friend Heliodorus on the death of his nephew Nepotian in 396 with words that could hardly be regarded as especially consoling!

I will say no more of the calamities of individuals; I come now to the frail fortunes of human life, and my soul shudders to recount the downfall of our age. For twenty years and more the blood of Romans has every day been shed between Constantinople and the Julian Alps. Scythia, Thrace, Macedonia, Thessaly, Dardania, Dacia, Epirus, Dalmatia, and all the provinces of Pannonia have been sacked, pillaged and plundered by Goths and Sarmatians, Quadians and Alans, Huns and Vandals and Marcomanni. How many matrons, how many of God's virgins, ladies of gentle birth and high position, have been made the sport of these beasts! Bishops have been taken prisoners, presbyters and other clergymen of different orders murdered. Churches have been overthrown, horses stabled at Christ's altar, the relics of the martyrs dug up.

*Sorrow and grief on every side we see
And death in many a shape.*

He concludes: "the Roman world is falling, and yet we hold our heads erect instead of bowing our necks. . . . Happy is Nepotian, for he does not see these sights nor hear these cries" (quoted by Gerald Bonner in *St. Augustine of Hippo: Life and Controversies*, p. 150).

Throughout most of Augustine's life, terrorism and barbarism had been on the increase, steadily eating like cancer into the entrails of the empire. The German peoples constituted an ever-increasing menace to the stability of the empire that would eventually sweep away all its foundations of law and order and solidarity, leaving in its place independent, yet still distinctively Romanized, barbarian kingdoms. The initial result of this was to be what history has called the Dark Ages. The long-term result was the creation of sovereign states in the Middle Ages culminating in the Hundred Years War. Jerome's letters mark the beginning of the end: a season of lawlessness, terrorism, and disintegration.

It was during the times of these "barbaric invasions" that the inconceivable occurred. On August 24, 410, an army of Goths led by Alaric, a nominal ally of Rome and even a general in the service of the Roman emperor, entered Rome and sacked and burned the ancient, sacred city for three days, spreading terrorism and barbarism right into the heart and soul of the empire. Pelagius, a monk from Britain whom we shall meet in another context later, was staying in Rome at the time. In a letter to a Roman lady, he gives us a firsthand account of the earth-shattering events:

Rome, the mistress of the world, shivered, crushed with fear, at the sound of the blaring trumpets and the howling of the Goths. Where, then, was the nobility? Where were the certain and distinct ranks of dignity? Everyone was mingled together and shaken with fear; every household had its grief and that all-pervading terror gripped us. Slave and noble were one. The same spectre of death stalked before us all.

—Letter to Demetria, 30

Jerome, in another one of his somewhat lugubrious letters, asked, "If Rome can perish, what can be safe?" It was the symbolic effect of the fall of Rome that was most powerful. The news running round the Western world was as much a force for terrorism as the event itself.

It is true that Rome was in reality no longer the political capital of the empire. Yet it was still the home of many leading figures of political society, and it symbolized Roman justice, Roman civilization, and the famous Pax Romana—the mortar that was supposed to hold the edifice of empire together and keep it standing for a thousand years.

Terrorism is in its nature more a matter of symbolism than of actual might. It is the recourse of the weak, of those unable to match strength with strength. The blows it strikes are usually more expressions of rage than they are effective military actions. Blowing up the Statue of Liberty, say, or Big Ben or the Arc de Triomphe would convey a stronger message than a conventional military engagement even on a much larger scale. It is hard for us to grasp the earthshaking significance that the fall of Rome had in the Late Antiquity. Roman culture and civilization represented to the world of Augustine the zenith of human achievement. Indeed, from their perspective, the Roman Empire embodied the climax of the ages. If it was to disintegrate as all empires had before it, what did this say about the shape and destiny of history? If Rome represented the high summer of human achievement, what was to follow? Was there nothing else to which the world could now look forward except a winter of despair and disaster?

Disaster, war, sudden death, and national calamities always bring religious questions to the surface among even the most urbane and secular minds. It would be hard to make sense of a sudden disintegration of the whole of Western civilization in our own day. We could be forgiven for believing that such a disintegration might in some sense herald the end of everything. Indeed, much of the millennium neurosis of our own day is fed by such a sense of disintegration in our contemporary culture; many today who are perplexed "with fear for what is coming upon the earth" eagerly turn to the prophets of doom and gloom.

Augustine witnessed this sense of disintegration and eagerly sought an appropriate response as a Christian, theologian, and bishop. His letters are full of it. Toward the end of 408 he wrote a long letter to the somewhat refined and otherworldly figure Paulinus of Nola, who at that time was not yet a bishop, was in fact living with his wife in just the kind of cultured retirement that Augustine had sought in his earlier life and of which his vocation to be a bishop had so quickly robbed him. He chided Paulinus for assuming that he could afford to be otherworldly, withdrawn from the upheavals and anxieties that were breaking loose throughout the known Western world. Nor did Augustine fail to point out to Paulinus that as bishop of Hippo his vocation compelled him to "live *among* men, for their benefit" and furthermore that in the climate of the times responsibility for leadership was falling upon the shoulders of men like himself who "are having to conduct the affairs of a whole people—not of the Roman people on earth, but of the citizens of the heavenly Jerusalem" (*Epistolae,* 95.5).

Double Citizenship

AUGUSTINE was alluding in his letter to Paulinus to the increasing sense of tension that he and many of his fellow bishops were feeling at the time. They held, as it were, a double citizenship.

As Christians, their citizenship was in heaven of course; in a real sense their baptism had made them aliens in a foreign land. Yet, since the last decade of the previous century, the church had gained more and more ground in leadership in the empire. For example, the victory Ambrose achieved over the liberal pleas of Symmachus in the previous century had encouraged succeeding generations of bishops to continue to press for the suppression of all public signs of paganism. The bishops had led the attack on the destruction of all the old ways of the old world. This was especially so in Africa, where many of the great pagan temples that had remained open "for the masterpieces that were there to be seen" were now closed. Public and private sacrifices to the pagan gods had been forbidden under the emperors Valentinian II and Theodosius. State financial support for the upkeep of pagan religious institutions had long since been withdrawn.

Augustine was clearly well-prepared and single-minded in his opposition to the remaining architecture of polytheism and other pagan superstitions marring the skylines of African cities. Preaching in Carthage one Sunday in June A.D. 401, he stirred up the congregation with passionate preaching against the stubborn resistance of paganism to the newly established Christian orthodoxy that now belonged to the official politics of the empire. He seized on a text from a psalm that had been sung during the course of the liturgy for the day— "Lord, who is like unto Thee?" This seemed as good a text as any with which to strike further blows against the residual pagan practices in Carthage. The temples dedicated to the pagan gods had been closed for more than two years, but it seemed to Augustine that pagan practices and paraphernalia were persisting.

He lost no opportunity to point out that in Rome the temples had been destroyed and the idols and statues with them. Why was it not the same in Carthage as in Rome? Augustine having used this phrase as a refrain, the excited congregation soon picked it up as well: "In Carthage as in Rome." His rhetoric reached its climax with a challenge to the congregation: "If the Roman gods have disappeared from Rome, why do they remain here? If they could walk they would answer that they had fled to this place. Think well, dear brethren, think well! I have said what I have said," concluded the wily preacher; "it is for you to draw the conclusions." At this point, we are told by the stenographers, wild applause broke out, and three times the congregation shouted as one man: "Dii Romani."

We know from a comment he made in a letter what pleasure Augustine derived from the devastation of pagan temples in the city where he preached on that topic with such power and passion. He describes with zest the devastation of these temples, noting that they were "in part completely fallen into ruin, in part pulled down, in part closed or used for some purpose other than their original one, the statues broken in pieces, burned, carried off or utterly destroyed." There was certainly not a drop of the liberal Symmachus's blood flowing in the veins of Augustine, the orthodox crusader of his day.

And now, the sack of Rome. How did such an event disturb the collective religious psyche of the empire? When public disaster strikes, the sheep look up to the shepherds for guidance, interpretation, and encouragement. Augustine, like every good preacher, held as it were the Bible in one hand and the newspaper in the other. After all, Christianity was at the helm of the empire in this time of peril. Augustine even went so far as to suggest that there had been a model Christian prince occupying the seat of power toward the close of the fourth century—Theodosius the Great. Rome had supported the established church legally in its battle against the Donatists and had taken its side in many controversies. Now see what happened!

The Signs of the Times

THE character of Augustine's mind and his sense of pastoral responsibility drove him to consider the signs of the times—for the sake of his congregation and for the sake of the wider public that by now looked to Hippo for intellectual and spiritual leadership to make sense of what was happening throughout the world.

Like every good teacher and preacher, in addressing his concerned audience he took an image that was ready at hand. Africa was, he suggested, very much a land of olive trees, in which there was no shortage of cheap, rough olive oil. Throughout summer the olive trees grew heavy with their plentiful crop of olives. Toward the end of the year, those olives would be beaten down from the trees and crushed for their oil in large presses. (The olive press was known as the *torcular,* and at this point in Augustine's ministry we find him often employing the *torcular* as a telling sermon illustration.) In some sense, he told them, history had reached the season for pressing. "The world reels under crushing blows, the old man is shaken out; the flesh is pressed, the spirit turns to clear flowing oil."

The events culminating in the sack of Rome, the signs of the times, called for a season when the flesh had to be disciplined, had to be pressed so that the spirit of renewal could flow like oil. The political and international events of his day constituted what Augustine perceived to be a spiritual challenge to the Christian church set within the history of the world, which in some sense was passing away.

The evidence of this passing away of former times was all around Augustine. On a long journey on horseback returning from Carthage in the autumn of 410, Augustine noticed a huge and unrepaired amphitheater beginning to crumble into ruin. There was no longer either the money or the the will to maintain the fabric of a society set upon decline. And so Augustine preached,

You are surprised that the world is losing its grip? That the world is growing old? Think of a man: he is born, he grows up, he becomes old. Old age has its many complaints: coughing, shaking, failing eyesight, anxious, terribly tired. A man grows old: he is full of complaints. The world is old: it is full of pressing tribulations. . . . Do not hold onto the old man, the world; do not refuse to regain your youth in Christ, who saves you: The world is passing away, the world is losing its grip, the world is short of breath. Do not fear, Thy youth shall be renewed as an eagle.

—Sermons, *81.8*

Volusianus, the gifted son of an established Roman family, used his political and literary influence to swell the tide of nostalgia for the golden days of Rome in the empire's latter days. The resurgence of literary and philosophical paganism he encouraged drew Augustine to the task of writing The City of God.

That was all right coming from the pulpit, but Augustine knew that he would be compelled to respond in print to the pertinent questions of a larger public. He knew in his bones that there were bigger issues that had to be dealt with, not just by his tongue but with his pen. He felt the Italian bishops were not giving a lead in this matter. Not in the best of health at the time when the blow struck in 410, he did not want at first to commit himself to another great literary undertaking. However, in addition to widespread dismay and the popular hysteria arising out of the sack of Rome, something more fundamental was occurring in the intellectual, philosophical, and cultural substructures of the day. It constituted a challenge to which Augustine almost compulsively responded, a challenge for which his whole life had in some ways been a preparation. It was as though it had been "for this very hour" that he had come to the office of bishop and teacher in the church of God.

Reaction and Challenge

AUGUSTINE was becoming increasingly aware of a neopagan intelligentsia that was stubbornly reasserting the religious practices and cultural symbols of the golden age of the empire now slipping away into the past. Volusianus personified for Augustine this reactionary movement, which was becoming conspicuous by the beginning of the fifth century. Volusianus was still only a young man, about thirty years old, whose family had estates at Tubursicubure—not very far from Hippo. It was an old, established Roman family that dutifully clung to the religion of their pagan fathers and forefathers. Their religious practices were part of their assertion and claim to be from the *ancien regime*. (In this, they were not unlike many old English Catholic families who after the Reformation retained a chapel and Catholic priest to say mass for the family.)

The world in which Volusianus lived as a young man was supposed to be, and in many ways was, a post-pagan world. He served emperors who were officially Christian. Nevertheless, the religion of the good old days held a special attraction for Volusianus, who was now the center of a literary circle that forged politics, literary interests, and religious practices together into a shield against the onslaught of Christianity.

A pagan reaction and revival was almost inevitable after the strong assertion of Christianity immediately following the Peace of Constantine. We find it most clearly expressed in one book of the time—*Saturnalia* by Macrobius. This book portrays the great Roman conservatives in their heyday (around 380). Not surprisingly, it features an old friend and adversary of Ambrose—Symmachus—as well as Praetextatus, the great pagan religious expert of his day, and Albinus, the father of young Volusianus. Macrobius depicts these men reasserting in their learned discussions all the values of the good old days, including a powerful (if somewhat nostalgic) reaffirmation of all the ancient religious practices. After all, he asserts, it was men like these, contending for these kind of values (pagan morality and philosophy at its best), who brought the empire to its height of glory. Drawing on all the great Platonists of their age—Plotinus, Porphyry, and indeed Cicero himself before them (just as Augustine had done before his conversion), they were able to uncover the bedrock of philosophy, religion, and metaphysics—the rock on which the empire was founded.

To such intellects as Volusianus, Christianity looked like a new import from outside of Roman history, tradition, and outlook. It had undermined the very foundations on which the empire had become great. If the empire were ever to recover its former glory, it would have to tap all its old roots—the old religion as well as the old culture, for they were in a real sense inseparable. And it seemed to many that it was high time to recapture some of the glory of the great old days before all these catastrophes swept everything away.

Augustine knew from his days in Rome and Milan something of this literary and philosophical neopaganism. After all, he had been the protégé of Symmachus. He had lectured to the sons of many of his friends and camp followers. It is not too cynical to say that in his early life and career Augustine had aspired to move in precisely such circles and to receive the approval and applause of these very men. He also knew that to such men, as to himself at one stage in his earlier pilgrimage, Christianity had appeared incapable of sustained intellectual combat with the experts and wise men of paganism. Christian apologetics often seemed to pale alongside the more impressive religious and philosophical manufacturings of the pagan world. Christians were often comparatively lightweight in their intellectual stamina and in their knowledge of classical Roman and Greek philosophy—the environment in which pagan religion had flourished.

The City of God: Magnum Opus

ALTHOUGH he was reluctant to undertake the massive project that the grave issues at hand clearly called for, Augustine knew in every fiber of his being that he was the man for the job. In the end, it was a responsibility (albeit burdensome) that he simply could not evade. Sermons and letters would not answer the challenge issued by Volusianus and others of his caliber. It would require nothing less than a major production: Augustine's magnum opus, *The City of God.*

In many ways the challenge struck right to the heart of Augustine's pride—nothing less than his reputation was now at stake. Peter Brown insists that the *City of God* is "the most self-conscious book that he [Augustine] ever wrote" (*Augustine of Hippo,* p. 303). It is certainly the longest! This was no tract or popular pamphlet. It was aimed at the aristocracy of literature and philosophy in Augustine's day and had to compare favorably with the literary output of Volusianus and his circle. The result, therefore, was a huge work, containing twenty-two books in all and aspiring to be nothing less than the greatest "apology of the church against paganism, the final justification of her teaching and historical position at the end of time, and before the whole world."

From the very beginning, while the ink was still wet on the parchment—even after the publication of just the first three books of the *City of God*—Augustine received rave reviews from around the empire. "I am in a quandary," wrote one admittedly sympathetic reviewer, "as to which to admire the most: the complete religious knowledge of a priest; the range of philosophical opinions; the fullness of its historical information; the charm of a grand style" (*Epistolae*, 154.2).

It has to be admitted, however, that many of the twenty-two books into which the *City of God* is divided have little to say to a general readership today. Twelve of the books develop Augustine's great thesis and theme—a tale of two cities. He contends that there are in effect two cities and not just one—two cities, one of God, the other of the world. "My task," he says, "is to discuss, to the best of my power, the rise, the development and the destined ends of the two cities, the earthly and the heavenly, the cities which we find, as I have said, interwoven, as it were, in this present transitory world, and mingled with one another" (*De Civitate Dei*, 11.1). The two cities are interwoven and mingled with one another in the field of history, says Augustine, but their citizens differ sharply, constituting in fact two different branches of the human race: "The one consists of those who live by human standards, the other of those who live according to God's will. . . . By two cities I mean two societies of human beings, one of which is predestined to reign with God for all eternity, the

other doomed to undergo eternal punishment with the Devil" (*De Civitate Dei*, 15.1).

Can the City of God be equated with the church then? No, that is not what Augustine has in mind. It is not as simple as that. The church is a temporal institution, and the City of God is more than that. Within the context of history, the two overlap, but the City of God will survive beyond history while the institutional church will not. The citizens of the City of God belong to that great sweep of the whole people of God from Adam to Christ and from Christ to our own day until the end of time. Intermingled with the people of God are those who belong to the institutional church and yet who will not end up in the City of God because they actually live by human standards. As Augustine puts it,

while the City of God is on pilgrimage in this world, she has in her midst some who are united with her in participation in the sacraments, but who will not join with her in the eternal destiny of the saints. Some of these are hidden: some are well-known, for they do not hesitate to murmur against God, whose sacramental sign they bear, even in the company of his acknowledged enemies. At one time they join his enemies in filling the theatres, at another they join with us in filling the churches.
—De Civitate Dei, *1.35*

With this perspective of the sweep and pilgrimage of history, Augustine is able to be confident that the City of God will be salvaged from history—even the history that includes the disintegration of the city and empire of Rome. Nothing will be lost that is of God. It will emerge triumphantly at the end of time, clearly vindicated and recognizable as the true City of God. So with

Botticelli's Augustine in Florence. Battle-scarred, the Bishop of Hippo retired to his library.
"I have resolved," he wrote, "to devote my time entirely, if the Lord will, to the labor of studies
pertaining to ecclesiastical writing: in doing which I think that I may, if it please the mercy of
God, be of some service even to future generations" (Epistolae, 151.13).

the church. It contains many anomalies and contradictions that throughout the pilgrimage of history will be seen for what they are—the evidences of citizens who are in fact of the other city, destined for ultimate destruction.

In many ways Augustine killed two birds with one stone when he wrote *The City of God*. He had to answer the challenge of Volusianus and his friends concerning the fate of Rome and its empire, but he also had to explain the destructive and evil elements in the church that had since the Peace of Constantine almost exactly a hundred years earlier increasingly become conformed to the human standards of the city of this world. In *The City of God* he rescues theology and a view of history from static categories formed by analysis in the context of some fixed point in history. He directs our attention instead to the end of all things: the solution to history lies in a point of convergence beyond history when all will be what it seems and when the two cities will stand clearly for what they are. The Roman Empire and the institutional church are, he says, little more than sieves in a process that at the end of the ages will have produced clearly defined and opposing categories. In the meantime, Augustine is happy to borrow from the parable of the wheat and the tares—"Let both grow together."

Vision and Glory

Wᴵᵀᴴ such a perspective, what was Augustine's view on the glory of Rome, the city and its empire? He acknowledged its glorious past, but he wished to make clear how that glory came about and equally how and why that glory was clearly coming to an end. There had been real discipline and spiritual goals at work in founding and establishing the great glory of Rome, he suggested. It was paganism with its later decadence that undermined the early discipline and genuinely spiritual goals. In Book Six, Augustine refuses to spare our blushes as he points to the poisonous sewage of filth and immorality in which Rome was perishing. Why did it all come to an end? "They were passionately devoted to glory; it was for this that they desired to live, for this they did not hesitate to die. This unbounded passion for glory, above all else, checked their other appetites. They felt it would be shameful for their country to be enslaved, but glorious for her to have dominion and empire; and so they set their hearts first on making her free, then on making her sovereign" (*De Civitate Dei*, 5.12). What a glorious mandate for cities and countries and empires: struggle first to be free from sin in order that they may truly be sovereign and rule responsibly over all.

Augustine labored on his magnum opus from 413 to 426. More and more things seemed to fall into place as the model of the two cities developed and extended in its application. Increasingly, however, there is a sort of fascination bordering on obsession in his vision of the goal of the true City of God that will be made evident at the end of time.

When Augustine was preaching once in Carthage toward the end of his life, he spoke of this growing fascination with the City of God—not with his magnum opus as such but with the goal and vision for all of history. "When, therefore, death shall be swallowed up in victory, these things will not be there; and there shall be peace—peace full and eternal. We shall be in a kind of city. Brethren, when I speak of that city, and especially

A fifteenth-century miniature illustrating Augustine's magnum opus, the City of God. *The city within contains the saints who have already entered heaven; the seven enclosures of the city without contain those who are preparing to enter the heavenly kingdom—or excluding themselves by practicing one of the seven deadly sins.*

when scandals grow great here, I just cannot bring myself to stop."

So it was with the book—he simply could not bring himself to stop writing it! For thirteen years, on and off he labored at this thesis of a lifetime and gave to the world his philosophy of history in a masterpiece that has secured for him the title of the greatest of the fathers in the Western church.

Reading the work, one cannot help but sense Augustine's fascination with and personal involvement in the image that dominates the book from cover to cover. By the time he had completed *The City of God* he was an old man, in his seventies, witnessing the collapse of the Christian church in Africa and apprehensive for the future of the Christian empire he had built up by God's grace at Hippo in almost forty years of his ministry. "And now, as I think, I have discharged my debt, with the completion, by God's help, of this huge work" (*De Civitate Dei,* 22.30).

The last chapter of his life, as we shall see, was free neither of controversy within nor combat without. He was a tired man, wearied by continuing controversies and worried by the approaching combat with barbarism that was nearing the walls of his own city—the city of Hippo.

There is much more going on in *The City of God* than just an assessment of competing philosophical and theological claims. In the concluding chapters Augustine speaks candidly of his aspirations to reach the peace and safety of that Eternal City about which he had written at such length. For he knew that while he was in Hippo, as bishop of that city, there would be no peace and no lasting security. The restlessness that was so evident in the

opening chapters of his life returned, though now for very different reasons. It is not that he did not know where to find rest as had been the case in his early life. Now he knew where that rest is to be found and where there is true and lasting peace. It was only a matter of when and how he would finally attain to it. He waited patiently to find peace and rest in the City of God: "We shall be still and see; we shall see and we shall love; we shall love and we shall praise. Behold what will be, in the end, without end! For what is our end but to reach that Kingdom which has no end."

CHAPTER TEN

THE LAST DAYS

Refugees across the Empire

AFTER the sack of Rome in 410 the Roman Empire was deeply unsettled. Refugees from Rome sought the security of the provinces. Some such refugees—many of them from the nobility of Rome—found their way across the Mediterranean to Africa, to the port of Hippo, to the very doorstep of Augustine's diocese and community. Of course, for such people who had been accustomed to the cultural climate of Rome and Italy, Africa was very much a backwater. Yet in times of terrorism and instability backwaters have the advantage of being less likely to attract the attention of an aggressor.

One of the refugees who arrived in Thagaste described Augustine's birthplace as "small and very poor." It was neither the size nor the poverty of provincial Africa that was to be its undoing, however. Proba, the widow of the richest man in the whole of the Roman Empire, turned up in Hippo and met the aging Augustine. Melania and Pinianus, two slightly dotty millionaires who had left Rome, sold much of their property, and given the proceeds to the poor, also visited Hippo and were set on by locals, who were always attentive to the possibility of receiving a rich patron as one of their priests.

To all these visitors, the petty squabbles of the church in Africa must have appeared strangely provincial and irrelevant set alongside the larger international problems of the empire. For it was indeed the case that the church in Africa was fiddling with theological niceties while Rome was literally burning at the hands of the terrorists. During the year of the crisis 410, most of Augustine's energies were drained by his crusade to Carthage to combat the Donatists. On any showing, the Dona-tist controversy was a somewhat petty ecclesiastical matter that should have been eclipsed by larger issues—not least by a concern for and commitment to mission among the Berber and Punic mountain villages and communities that were so numerous in Numidia and throughout the African province.

Furthermore, there were the larger issues associated with the church's care for a crumbling society and a disintegrating empire. Its doors were by now not only open but off their hinges—wide open to the barbarian invaders who were to sweep across the empire gutting the Christian church within a generation, and only a hundred years later replacing it in large part with the militant religion of Islam.

The British Heretic Pelagius

YET, equally relevant, and potentially even more destructive, was the rise of a new liberal laity composed of men and women of wealth and high social background who still clung to the security of the empire, men and women who were determined to speak of mankind and its destiny in terms that were strangely optimistic.

It was among this class of cultured, even prosperous Christian laypeople who had not known the age of persecution personally and who now exercised considerable influence in the crumbling empire that Pelagius, a layman from Britain, conducted his somewhat genteel Bible classes in Rome at the beginning of the fifth century. His lectures in these classes formed the basis of an early work—*Expositions of the Letters of St. Paul.* His style was

Pelagius, a contemporary of Augustine whose heretical teachings touched points of doctrine and experiences at the very heart of the saint's faith

exceedingly effective: he wrote in the form of letters of exhortation, and he was widely read in the circles that also prized Augustine's works. Early on, Augustine himself admired the style in which Pelagius wrote: his letters and exhortations were "well written," Augustine freely acknowledged, and went "straight to the point."

Yet, as Augustine knew, style was no substitute for content. What was Pelagius really saying? He was saying in effect what from time to time (when things are going well for us) we are all tempted to say: mankind is coming of age! All that debilitating and depressing doctrine about the Fall of man and the inherent sinfulness of man—surely, it was possible to go beyond that and see a more optimistic future for the human race. Pelagius wanted to live and write for men and women who were committed to making a change for the better. At the outset he had expressed his dislike of the passage in the *Confessions* in which Augustine says to his God, "Command what you will." Pelagius believed the phrase stemmed from the passions, the root of mankind's problems. The phrase seemed to him to suggest that God's commands are somehow arbitrary, even absurd, and it certainly did not seem to him that it constituted a mature response to the commands of the majestic Lawgiver. He contended that such terms as *sin* and *grace* were too emphatic, too cosmic; the human condition, he insisted, is more a matter of personal peccadillos and failings than of world-rending sin.

Pelagius never doubted that with God's grace human beings could attain perfection. He went so far as to urge his self-made disciples to have a new confidence in their ability to achieve that perfection: "Since perfection is possible for man, it is

obligatory" he once counseled a nun. "Whenever I have to speak of laying down rules for behavior and conduct of the holy life," he said, "I always point out, first of all, the power and functioning of human nature, and show what it is capable of doing . . . lest I should seem to be wasting my time, by calling on people to embark on a course which they consider impossible to achieve."

Pelagianism

SOMETIMES called the Englishmen's heresy, Pelagianism (as history came to know it) is in fact a dangerous fallacy in the diagnosis of mankind's condition. When Pelagius published his pamphlet *On Nature,* every bone in Augustine's body told him that while this well-spoken British layman from Rome might be no more than a hair's breadth distant from traditional scriptural theology, he was in his essential approach light-years distant from Christian orthodoxy.

Pelagius visited Hippo briefly on his way to the Holy Land, and he missed meeting Augustine by what is against the backdrop of history the smallest margin of time. In reality, though, they could never have met and agreed; they had no common ground.

Few things were nearer Augustine's own personal experience than the issue of nature and grace. He never forgot (and refused to allow subsequent history ever to forget) the wayward, delinquent, and basically depraved nature of humankind. He insisted that mankind needed salvation, not perfection; redemption, not just education; sanctification, not self-improvement. Augustine took on Pelagius not only because he had a nose for controversy for its own sake but also because the issues involved struck at the very heart of his conversion experience. In many ways the personal flesh-and-blood story of the work of grace that he presents in the *Confessions* contains all the elements that would come to the fore in his theological controversy with Pelagius.

In the year 415, Augustine wrote his famous treatise *Nature and Grace*. In it he delivers a succinct and brilliantly orthodox message that should be framed and displayed prominently by everyone to this day, particularly at those moments in history when confidence in human goodness and strength insinuates itself into the diagnosis of the human condition:

Without God we cannot,

Without us, he will not.

Augustine walks confidently between the two sides of this paradox. On the one hand is the abyss of pietism and quietism—the belief that we can do absolutely nothing at all and that we simply have to accept the process of redemption passively. On the other hand is the abyss of Pelagianism, the contention that we can be perfect in our own strength and that everything depends upon us. Augustine affirmed both aspects of the paradox, accommodating the tension between them without toppling into error on either side. Preaching on nature and grace once, he said, "He who created you without your help, will not save you without your cooperation" (*Sermons,* 169.13) It was with words such as these that Augustine made his case against Pelagius.

In the end, Pelagius was condemned as a heretic by African councils at Carthage and Mileve in 416 (largely led and influenced by the aging bishop from Hippo). The following year, Pope Innocent I endorsed the condemnations and declared Pelagius excommunicated. Although Pelagius contested this judgment at a hearing in Rome, a council at Carthage in 418 upheld the condemnation of Pelagius and Pelagianism, and the position was finally and permanently endorsed by Rome and engraved upon the pages of history. Beyond this we know nothing of the comings and goings of this famous and illustrious biblical teacher and spiritual guide, not even where he died or was buried.

Augustine and the African church made sure that Pelagianism was quashed, though the name and message of Pelagius are, like the poor, always with us. Pelagianism is endemic in all those chapters of history when it seems that mankind might not be so bad after all. On the whole, we hear more Pelagianism preached from pulpits than ever we hear Augustinianism. Preachers speak of success and achievement; breakfast Bible study classes for businessmen and Rotary Club luncheons are frequently infected by the virus of sensible human virtues that, if properly identified, would bear the name of Pelagius. In fact, in spite of so much evidence to the contrary in our daily newspapers and in our own lives, the temptation to play down human weakness and play up mankind's strengths and virtues is ever with us—at least until an Auschwitz or a Dachau recalls us to a more modest and less optimistic picture of the human race and its potential.

As the years drew on for Augustine, he was emerging as a battle-scarred but triumphant crusader for Christian orthodoxy. It is interesting that most of the works he wrote toward the end of his life were inspired by events and people who challenged Christian orthodoxy as he saw it. Always we must remember that Augustine saw it through the perspective of the experiences of frailty and moral weakness he had acknowledged so candidly in the *Confessions.*

It was inevitable, therefore, that Julian of Eclanum and Augustine should soon find themselves in very opposite corners of the ring and that once again Augustine would find himself engaged in theological combat and controversy. Until almost the day of his death in 430, Augustine never put down the theological cudgels in his battle for Christian orthodoxy. In those latter days, he was a formidable adversary on any showing.

Julian of Eclanum

As we have noted, Pelagianism survived its prime mover to remain a force wherever the climate of opinion is temperate and manners and intellect are well-developed. Pelagianism was tailor-made for Julian of Eclanum, who came from a family of noble birth, the son of Bishop Memorius. A priest himself, Julian married the daughter of another bishop. There was money, culture, manners, and education in the whole of his family, which exhibited its gentle Christian virtues without self-conscious straining or obvious austerity. In such a person as Julian, who became at about the age of thirty the Bishop of Eclanum in Apulia, Pelagianism found a most able, eloquent, and determined defender. Exiled from Italy for continually championing the views of Pelagius, he found refuge in the East. He traveled widely throughout the church for twenty years castigating all opponents of Pelagianism in general and Augustine of Hippo in particular.

In the first place, Julian pitted his genteel and sophisticated Italian background against the provincial background of Augustine and the strident and militant version of orthodox Christianity that Augustine had so long and so successfully championed. As far as he was concerned, Augustine was all "the African." It was as though Julian was waging another Punic War, this time in the name of theology. He contended that men like Augustine and Alypius (the latter was well-known in Italy as a result of his frequent diplomatic missions to the Court of Ravenna) were propagating a severe form of Christianity that suppressed with harsh discipline all opponents of what was essentially a perverted form of Christianity. First the Donatists and then the Pelagians—to Julian and others of liberal persuasion, African Christianity loomed as a repressive force in the Christian church. "The helm of reason," said Julian, "has been wrenched from the church, so that opinions of the mob can sail ahead with all flags flying."

Indeed, speaking in the name of reason and moderation, Julian made an accusation against Augustine that virtually all subsequent critics of the Bishop of Hippo have echoed. Had not Augustine spent many years under the influence of Manichaean teachers? Surely all his talk about the Fall of man and original sin can be best explained in reference to this early influence. He once advocated Manichaeism, but, having rejected it, he could never deal reasonably with the basic issues again. He retained a Manichaean split in his perceptions, and he became obsessed with the doctrine of the depravity of man.

From 419 onward, Julian, writing from the comparative leisure of his exile, produced various manifestos, often in the form of open letters, and no fewer than twelve volumes castigating the views of Augustine. Neither Augustine nor Julian should have been proud of the depths to which each sank at various points in the fierce and often vitriolic contest. Augustine was an old man, somewhat wearied and scarred by his years as a campaigner in the field of the battle for orthodoxy. Julian was much younger, exhibiting precisely that precocious tenacity that characterized Augustine in his own early years—notably in his correspondence with another old man, Jerome. Nevertheless, it must be granted that at one point in his dealings with Julian, Augustine displayed a genuine pastoral and loving (if somewhat patronizing) care. "My dear son, Julian," he wrote,

> *I have not forgotten your father, Memorius, of blessed memory with whom I was united by a close friendship through letters. It was he that inspired me with a tenderness for you. As for me, in virtue of the tenderness I have for you and which, with the grace of God, no insult will ever tear from my heart, I wish ardently, Julian, my dearest son, that by a better and stronger youth, you will triumph over yourself and that a sincere and true piety will make you renounce your ambitious and completely human desire which leads you to insist upon your own opinion, whatever it be, precisely because it is your opinion. . . . If the counsel I give you displeases you, act as you see fit. If you agree to correct yourself, as I most ardently wish, I will be filled with joy.*
>
> —Contra Julianus, 3. 1

Needless to say, Augustine was not filled with joy and Julian did not correct himself. The battle raged more furiously and less charitably.

Julian very evidently had a first-class mind, an eloquent and persuasive style, and he knew exactly where the Achilles heel was to be discovered in all of Augustine's arguments. Augustine, in contending for original sin as the foundation of human nature, was compelled by the force of his own argument to exempt no one from the curse of original sin—not even babies. Had not Augustine himself written many years previously about sin in babies in the opening chapters of his *Confessions*? "For in Your sight no man is free from sin, not even a child who has lived only one day on earth." And again: "I have myself seen jealousy in a baby and know what it means" (*Conf.*, 1.7). This gave Julian just the chance he needed. "Who was it," he demanded,

> who declared the innocent guilty, who was so heartless, so harsh, so oblivious of God and justice, who was so barbaric a tyrant, deserving the hatred of the human race, by failing to spare not only those who had not sinned, but even those who were incapable of sinning? Who is this person who punishes the innocent? When you answer "God" you give us a real shock. . . . The same God, you say, who commends His love towards us, who loved us and did not spare his own Son, but gave him up for us. He it is who passes this verdict, who persecutes newborn babies and assigns infants to eternal flames, infants whom he knows are incapable of either good or evil. What a cruel, blasphemous pernicious belief! You have departed so far from piety, from culture, even from plain common sense, as to believe that your God is guilty of injustice.

Fierce Controversy to the End

AUGUSTINE could see that there was no ground for reconciliation and was smarting from the wounds inflicted by such verbal blows. He took Julian on line for line and blow for blow—but he made his case not by contesting "culture" with culture or "common sense" with common sense but rather by calling on the full arsenal of Scripture, dictating late into the night to his secretaries his refutations of his opponent's plausible challenges. "Who are you, a man, to answer back to God?" (Rom. 9:20). "Truly, truly, I say to you, unless one is born of water and the Spirit, he cannot enter the kingdom of God" (John 3:5). It was to text after text from Scripture that Augustine appealed as he chiseled out an orthodox, scriptural doctrine of the nature of man.

Augustine maintained with Paul that the Fall had infected the whole cosmic order. That was the bad news. But he also stressed the good news of redemption, which likewise extends to the whole universe, with humanity as the hinge on which history itself turns. "As in Adam all die, so also in Christ shall all be made alive" (1 Cor. 15:22).

We in our post-Freudian age would do well to reflect upon Augustine's contentions, which have become the teaching of the whole church. Psychological insights have finally rescued all informed opinion from any residual sentimentality about babies and little children. There is enough rage within even a little baby to unhinge the universe! Indeed, the roots of mankind's problems are increasingly being located in precisely that chapter of our lives; contemporary insight suggests that a baby is anything but harmless. The years of infancy are the most formative—and hence potentially the most destructive—years of our life.

In any case, Augustine argues that all of us, the very young and the very old alike, are under the affliction of sin, which is patently evident in the whole fiber of the created order. But this bad news is balanced by the good news that grace, received into the universe through conscious and informed faith, has the power to go to the roots of our affliction and repair the damage. Both answer and problem are universal in their implication. Where Julian appealed to man's sentimentality, Augustine appealed to God's pragmatism. Where Julian appealed to human speculation, Augustine appealed to God's revelation.

And between the two there was a great gulf fixed. We now read what flowed from the pen of Augustine with the knowledge that in the end he won the victory on behalf of the church. From that vantage point, it is not difficult to lose sympathy with him and view his writings against Julian as extreme and overplayed. But when he was writing, it was by no means clear that the victory would be his—and the stakes were very high indeed. We have to remember that he was conducting important strategic theological warfare and that he won for the church territory it sorely needed at the time and will continue to need until the end of time.

Predestination

As the years drew on, Augustine became increasingly inflexible in his doctrine of grace. What was bred in the bone of the early years of his apostasy and intemperance came out in the flesh of his apostolic zeal in his last years and writings. In 426, when Augustine was seventy-two, two young monks from the monastery at Hadrumetum, on the coast of what we call today Tunisia, traveled specially to Hippo to talk with him. They told him plainly that his writings against both Pelagius and Julian had led to deep divisions of opinion in their monastery (divisions that were replayed in the sixteen-century battle between Calvinism and Catholicism). Originally the two monks had intended only a brief visit, but Augustine insisted they stay on with him at Hippo and engage in discussions and deliberations that would help him to write his great apology *Grace and Free Will*.

Augustine was now pushing hard on one side of the paradox—the assertion that grace is God's un-merited and free gift and that it is his alone to give. Augustine knew in his own life that he had no strength that had not been given to him by God. In *Grace and Free Will* he formalized the theology implicit in the *Confessions*. Yet he emphasized God's initiative in our redemption so much that he opened the door of theology inevitably upon another extreme position—the position of predestination later identified with Calvinism.

The visiting monks told Augustine that some of their brothers were asking "Why is it my fault if I don't have what I have not received from him, when he alone gives it?" The logical consequence of Augustine's position would seem to be that God must be the only sinner. And yet Augustine never took his argument to this conclusion, and it is not fair for us to do so. He was taking up a position in an argument that was already loaded against him, not trying to show us some objective and logical conclusion. He had to overstate his case precisely because it had been so understated and overlooked in the first place—and this in a climate in which balance, law and order, and justice were rapidly disappearing.

It is important to remember that in his last days Augustine carried on his theological warfare against the backdrop of increasing warfare of another kind. Barbarism had already reached the borders of Numidia and was soon to be at the gates of Hippo. Augustine was caught in the crossfire of both wars.

The Vandals Are Coming

THERE were no two ways about it: the Vandals were coming. They were coming to Africa, pouring out of southern Spain under the leadership of a remarkable and powerful commander named Genseric—eighty thousand of them in all, crossing the Straits of Gibraltar and entering Africa by the western province of Mauretania, only a thousand miles or so west of Hippo. By 429 there could be little doubt that eventually all the provinces of Africa would be overrun by these hordes.

Alypius, Augustine, and many of the other bishops turned to the Roman general Boniface in the hope that he would protect and deliver Numidia. Boniface, who had recently been made a count, was prevented by matrimonial bereavement and other difficulties from responding swiftly or powerfully enough to keep the barbarians out of Numidia. Nevertheless, Augustine delivered a challenge to the count on behalf of the province:

What shall I say of the devastation of Africa by hordes of African Barbarians to whom no resistance is offered, while you are engrossed with such embarrassments in your own circumstances that you are taking no measures for arresting this calamity? Who would have believed, after Boniface had become a count of the empire and had been placed in command in Africa with so large an army and with such great authority, that the same man who formerly as tribune kept all these barbarous tribes in peace by storming their strongholds and menacing them with his small band of brave confederates, should now have suffered the Barbarians to be so bold, and to encroach so far, to destroy and plunder so much, to turn into deserts such vast regions once

densely peopled? Where were any found who did not predict that as soon as you obtained the authority of Count, the African hordes would not only be checked, but made tributaries to the Roman empire? And now you yourself perceive how completely the event has disappointed men's hopes!

As it happened, Augustine had turned to the wrong source for protection. The count no longer enjoyed the total support of Rome, and in any case Rome was no longer the efficient hub of the empire that it had once been. In desperation, Count Boniface took a chance and invited Genseric to cross with his eighty thousand from the beaches of Andalusia in Spain into the province of Mauretania in order to join forces with him against the African Vandals. Not surprisingly, this only made things worse.

It was only a thousand miles from Mauretania to Hippo, and it was not long before Augustine's biographer Possidius began describing the attacks and counterattacks of Vandals and barbarians swarming through Mauretania and then from there into Numidia.

And now there appeared in a short time great forces of the Vandal army with whom were associated Alans and Goths and people of other races, all armed with spears and exercised in war. They crowded the sea in ships from Spain and, passing into Africa, spread over the land, penetrating into every part of Mauretania and even into our province and district. They perpetrated all the cruelties and atrocities imaginable: robbery, murder, torturings, burnings, and innumerable other barbarities, so that the country became depopulated. They respected neither age nor sex nor priest nor ministers

GENSERIC'S VANDALS IN ITALY.

Genseric's Vandals in Italy. It did not take long for the Vandal forces to sweep through Northern Africa. The end of Roman Africa coincided almost to the day with the end of Augustine's life.

of God nor church buildings. Marauding and destroying came these ferocious hordes.
                                    —*Life of Augustine, 28*

The end of Roman Africa had come—an end that coincided almost exactly to the day with the end of Augustine's life.

Putting His House in Order

AUGUSTINE'S health had been failing. He knew that like Valerius of old he now needed help in the diocese. On September 26, 426, he called together his clergy and congregation in the basilica of Peace to make a solemn decision for the future of the diocese. He nominated the priest Eraclius to be his successor and then proceeded to say,

In this life, we are all bound to die; and for everyone, his last day is always uncertain. Yet, as babies, we can look forward to being boys; and, as boys, to youth; as youths, to being grownup; as young men, to reaching our prime; and in our prime, to growing old. Whether this will happen is uncertain, but there is always something to look forward to. But an old man has no further stage of life before him. Because God wished it, I came to this town in my prime. I was a young man then; now I have grown old.

Then he sat down, and, in accordance with the practice of Valerius, the successor Eraclius was summoned to preach while the old bishop remained seated on his raised throne. Eraclius opened with telling humility and humor: "The cricket chirps," he said, "the swan is silent."

The old monastic bishop and pastor lived out his final days in spiritual and physical pain. Yet he lived at the end of his life as he had begun it after his baptism—in community. "Under Bishop Augustine, everyone who lives with him, lives the life described in the acts of the apostles."

He had become a name and an authority throughout the church. His community at Hippo was frequently visited by people from throughout the church who came to seek his advice. He continued to offer such advice in letters, books, and sermons. One pressing question as the churches in Mauretania and increasingly in Numidia came under the attack of the barbarians was whether the bishops and the clergy should flee or stay. Possidius reports that Augustine counseled all who asked him that they should stay as long as there were Christians in need of the ministry of Word and sacrament. His advice was not without its qualifications, but it was basically the advice of a shepherd and pastor who refused to desert the flock.

As the Vandals pressed ever closer to Hippo and Augustine pressed ever closer to the end of his days on earth, he made a survey of the books he had dictated and published, some in the early days of his conversion when he was still a layman, some as a priest, and some as a bishop. Whenever he found anything in them that he had dictated or written when he had had comparatively little knowledge and understanding of Christian tradition and that was not in accordance with the church's mind, he censored and corrected it himself. "In this way," Possidius tells us "he wrote two volumes entitled *A Survey of My Books*"—what we now know as the *Retractions* (*Life of St. Augustine*, 28).

He was putting his house in order and preparing to die. He spent long hours in his library working and reviewing. "Above all," writes Peter Brown "it was the library itself that claimed his attention. On the shelves, in the little cupboards that were the bookcases of the late Roman men, there lay ninety-three of his own works, made up of two hundred thirty-two little books, sheaves of his letters, and, perhaps cupboards crammed with anthologies of his sermons, taken down by the stenographers of his admirers" (*Augustine of Hippo*, 1967).

142

A stained glass window in the basilica in Hippo depicting Augustine dying. The restless heart finally found rest on August 28 in the year of our Lord 430.

The Siege of Hippo

THE city of Hippo came under siege, a siege that was to last until eleven months after Augustine's death. "One day, when we happened to be at table with him," Possidius tells us, "and they were talking about the war and the siege, Augustine said to those around him: 'You ought to know that in these days of disaster for us my prayer to God is that he will either consent to liberate this besieged city or, if he thinks otherwise, will give his servants strength to go through what he wills for them or, so far as I am concerned, will take me from this world'" (*Life of St. Augustine*, 29). Presumably God indeed did think otherwise: the siege continued and Augustine drew close to death.

"Right up to his last illness," Possidius reassures us, Augustine continued to preach "God's word in the church unceasingly, vigorously, and powerfully, with sound mind and sound judgment" (*Life of St. Augustine*, 31). But in August of 430 he suddenly fell ill with a fever. It would seem that he knew he was about to die, for at the last there was a strange reversal in his habits. He who had demanded and needed community and human fellowship all his life now asked that he be left alone.

"So as not to have his thoughts distracted by anyone," concludes Possidius, "about ten days before his death he asked those of us who were with him not to let anyone go in to him, except at the times when the doctors came to see him or food was brought to him. This was attended to and carried out, and during the whole of that time he gave himself to prayer" (*Life of St. Augustine*, 31).

Requiescat in Pace

WE know the content of some of his last prayers because he had requested that "those Psalms of David which are especially penitential" were to be copied out. "When he was very weak, [he] used to lie in bed, facing the wall where the sheets of paper were put up, gazing at them and reading them and copiously and continuously weeping as he read." For as he once preached, "Whoever does not want to fear let him probe his inmost self. Do not just touch the surface; go down into yourself; reach into the farthest corner of your heart."

So, still searching, still seeking in the innermost corners of that restless heart, Augustine, Bishop of Hippo, at last found rest in his death on August 28, A.D. 430.

He had written significantly at the conclusion of his spiritual autobiography this prayer:

In that eternal sabbath you will rest in us, just as now you work in us. The rest that we shall enjoy will be yours, just as the work that we now do is your work done through us. But you, O Lord, are eternally at work and eternally at rest. It is not in time that you see or in time that you move or in time that you rest: yet you make what we see in time; you make time itself and the repose which comes when time ceases.

—Conf., *13.37*

At last the restless heart had found its rest in God. Finally he was to test the truth of what he had written some years before: "Our home is your eternity."

EPILOGUE

POSSIDIUS tells us that Augustine left no will, for "as one of God's poor he had nothing to leave," although he goes on to say that "It was a standing order that the library of the church and all the books should be carefully preserved for posterity." Then in the closing chapter of that biography, Possidius quotes from a secular poet:

Traveler, would you like to know
How poets live on after death?
As you read aloud, it is I who speak;
Your voice is sounded by my breath.
— The Life of St. Augustine, 31

There can be no doubt that Augustine has continued to "live on after death" in his many vigorous sentences and powerful paragraphs, which have continued over the centuries to be sounded by the breath of our saint both in the church and in the world at large. But in the days immediately following his death, it seemed as though everything he had stood for was destroyed.

As it turned out, Augustine was the last bishop of Hippo. The city was deserted by its inhabitants and burned to the ground by the Vandals. The only thing that escaped was Augustine's library. Four years later, Carthage itself fell to the Vandals, and Genseric became master of the Mediterranean, eventually sacking Rome yet again. The church in North Africa (Donatist, Arian, and orthodox Christian alike) was destroyed. The country fell back into a desolate barbarism. In a hundred years, Arabs poured in from the east bringing with them a new language and a new religion—Islam.

Augustine was spared the pain of seeing the final destruction of the city he had loved and served for so many years, including the basilica in which he had preached so powerfully and so persuasively. When he died, there were something like five hundred Catholic bishops in the province. Less than twenty years later there were only eighteen left in all of North Africa. It was not long before Roman rule, the Latin tongue, and the Christian religion had vanished from Hippo and the surrounding country. Hippo itself disappeared; crops were planted on its former site, animals grazed over it, and new houses were built on top of it—houses in which Latin was no longer spoken and in which Christ was no longer honored. In the nineteenth century the French occupied Algeria and built a cathedral dedicated to Augustine on the hill overlooking the ancient site of Hippo (now called Annaba). Today no more than about three hundred Catholic families live in Annaba and the surrounding area.

History tells us that a group of African bishops took the body of Augustine with them when they were fleeing from the Vandals and that it was subsequently deposited in Sardinia, where it remained until the eighth century. Then, on payment of gold equalling the weight of Augustine's body, a king of Lombardy brought it to Pavia, where it was buried. (Augustine was literally worth his weight in gold!) On October 1, 1695, a white marble sarcophagus was discovered in Pavia, and today in the church of Ciel D'oro at Pavia pilgrims can visit the shrine of St. Augustine.

The right arm (the arm used presumably in all that writing, to say nothing of the many blessings he gave as bishop) is retained in the cathedral at Annaba, and the windows around the church there tell in somewhat romantic nineteenth-century fashion the story of his life.

Humanly speaking, Augustine should have been

Right, the Augustine tree in modern-day Souk Ahras—a poor reminder, perhaps, of the local boy who made good, and yet a living reminder

Below, a plaque identifying Augustine's tomb

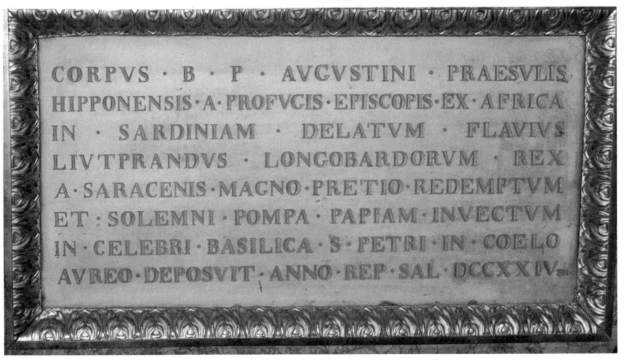

CORPVS · B · P · AVGVSTINI · PRAESVLIS
HIPPONENSIS · A · PROFVGIS · EPISCOPIS · EX · AFRICA
IN · SARDINIAM · DELATVM · FLAVIVS
LIVTPRANDVS · LONGOBARDORVM · REX
A · SARACENIS · MAGNO · PRETIO · REDEMPTVM
ET · SOLEMNI · POMPA · PAPIAM · INVECTVM
IN · CELEBRI · BASILICA · S · PETRI · IN · COELO
AVREO · DEPOSVIT · ANNO · REP · SAL · DCCXXIV

Above, *the basilica at Hippo*
Left, *Augustine's tomb in Pavia*

long dead and buried and largely forgotten. Much of his writing is frankly tedious and certainly bears the limitations implicit in the axioms of the age in which he lived. "Like all his contemporaries, he, too, was filled with a naive belief in miracles, and like most of his contemporaries with a taste for philosophy, he found it easier to give his unqualified assent to the value of invisible truth than to that of the visible world by which he was surrounded."

A Man for All Seasons

NEVERTHELESS, there are places where Augustine breaks loose from his age and becomes a man for all seasons—most obviously in his reflections, in his willingness to probe the depths of human nature. He does this most convincingly because he is not afraid to go deep within himself. Plumbing these depths, he strikes chords that resonate with similar depths in human nature sixteen hundred years later. The superficial will, like our skin, show age most evidently. It is the inner depths that change the least and that persistently speak the language of the ages.

In the first ten books of the *Confessions* we find the words of a man who was sensitive to evolution and development long before Darwin or Newman, who probed the subconcious and evaluated the world of dreams long before Freud or Jung. Augustine knew the darkness and depravity of human nature and refused to let us be unmindful of that potential for destruction within each one of us. It is one thing to be optimistic about mankind's achievements when the days are sunny; we need a

theology and a spirituality for the bleak days as well, for the darkest nights of revolution, terrorism, and the demonic forces of a Dachau or an Auschwitz.

Catholic and Protestant theologians alike turn to Augustine to vindicate their theses; political theorists and historians of Western thought cannot with integrity exclude this saint from their syllabus, however secularized they might seek to become. In philosophy he takes his place with Plato and Aristotle. There is indeed something very universal about this saint which ensures that he will endure.

His Voice in the Church

AND yet we need to heed again the words of Possidius, who in the last chapter of his biography tells us that "we shall profit most from Augustine when we hear him speak in church." It is in his words addressed to the people of God that he has the most to say to us.

He was at one and the same time an evangelist and a churchman. He loved the Scriptures. In an age like our own, torn between fundamentalist and liberal attitudes toward Scripture, Augustine said quite bluntly, "A plague on both your houses!" He loved Scripture, preached it, marked it, learned it, and made it a part of himself. It was his love of Scripture that made him a preacher. So he recalls the church in every season to be faithful in preaching and teaching. It was from a preacher and a teacher (Ambrose of Milan) that he learned all this; in his turn he taught it to all who followed him— perhaps most significantly to all those members of his community who in their turn became bishops.

His voice in the church today would surely constitute a serious summons (not least to the bishops of the church) to give new attention, commitment, and obedience to the Word of God revealed to us through the words of Scripture.

Yet at the same time he was a churchman. He knew that as an apostle he carried in his person the gospel: he was a walking sacrament, a pastor, a spiritual guide, a man of prayer, and a man of community. In his formative years he found a model bishop in the person of Ambrose; in his later years he sought to renew and refresh the image of the episcopate, cutting loose from the secularized models so evident in his day and recasting it in the mold of the gospel-bearing apostolic figure of the bishop.

He is an episcopal figure but he is never prelatical. "Among you I am a Christian; for you I am a bishop." For the base on which his episcopacy was founded was his baptism. Even his life in community was nothing more than a serious attempt to live out the implications of what took place on that Easter eve in Milan in 387. Everything in his Christian discipleship as well as in his episcopal duties flowed from those baptismal waters in which he had been submerged in his thirty-third year. Evangelist, churchman, bishop, and saint—and the great doctor of the church.

Yet Augustine is no angel: he is a saint. He points us not to himself, with all his failings, but to the God of abundant grace. He concludes his *Confessions* at the point where any record of sanctity should always conclude: "In prayer and adoration." Let his last word in the *Confessions* be ours also.

What man can teach another to understand this truth?
What angel can teach it to an angel?
What angel can teach it to a man?
We must ask it of you, O Lord God, seek it in you;
We must knock at your door.
Only then shall we receive what we ask and find what we seek;
Only then will the door be open to us.

—Conf., *13.38*

SELECTIVE BIBLIOGRAPHY

This bibliography is necessarily highly selective—as selective as the scholarship of the author is limited!

It is intended as a guide to beginning and enthusiastic study of the saint and bishop of Hippo. For further scholarly pursuit of this subject, readers are referred to the bibliography in the back of Peter Brown's biography, listed below.

Works by Augustine

Against the Academicians [Contra Academicos]. Milwaukee: Marquette University Press, 1957.

City of God. Translated by Henry Bettenson. 1972. Reprint. Harmondsworth: Penguin Books, 1984.

Confessions. Translated by R. S. Pine-Coffin. 1961. Reprint. Harmondsworth: Penguin Books, 1966.

Earlier Writings. Edited by J. H. S. Burleigh. Philadelphia: Westminster Press, 1953.

Later Works. Edited by John Burnaby. Philadelphia: Westminster Press, 1955.

Rule of St. Augustine, with Introduction and Commentary. London: Darton, Longman & Todd, 1984.

Selected Writings. New York: Paulist Press, 1984.

Works about Augustine

Bonner, Gerald. *St. Augustine of Hippo: Life and Controversies.* Revised edition. Norwich: Canterbury Press, 1986.

Brown, Peter. *Augustine of Hippo.* London: Faber & Faber, 1972.

_____. *The Cult of the Saints.* London: SCM Press, 1981.

_____. *The Making of Late Antiquity.* Cambridge: Harvard University Press, 1978.

_____. *Religion and Society in the Age of Augustine.* London: Faber & Faber, 1972.

_____. *Society and the Holy in Late Antiquity.* London: Faber & Faber, 1982.

Chadwick, Henry. *Augustine.* Oxford: Oxford University Press, 1986.

Evans, G. R. *Augustine on Evil.* Cambridge: Cambridge University Press, 1982.

Marcus, R. A. *Christianity in the Roman World.* London: Thames & Hudson, 1974.

Possidius, *Life of St. Augustine.* Translated by F. H. Hoare. The Western Fathers Series. London: Sheed & Ward, 1954.

Rowe, Trevor. *St. Augustine: Pastoral Theologian.* London: Epworth Press, 1974.

Smith, Warren Thomas. *Augustine: His Life and Thought.* Atlanta: John Knox Press, 1980.

Taylor, David Bentley. *Augustine: Wayward Genius.* London: Hodder & Stoughton, 1980.

Teselle, Eugene. *Augustine the Theologian.* New York: Herder & Herder, 1970.

Van der Meer, Frederick. *Augustine: The Bishop.* London: Sheed & Ward, 1961.

About the Illustrations

The author and publisher gratefully acknowledge permission from the following sources to reproduce illustrations in this volume:

Historical Picture Service for illustrations on pages 47, 127, 132, and 134;

North Wind Picture Archives for the frontispiece art and illustrations on pages 36 and 141;

and

Religious News Service for the illustration on page 543.

All of the remaining photographs were taken by the Reverend Charles Bewick.

About the Book

Editorial Work: T. A. Straayer
Design and Production: Joel Beversluis
Text Type: 12 on 13 Horley Old Style
Typesetter: The Composing Room of Michigan, Inc.
Separations: Black Dot Graphics
Printing and Binding: R. R. Donnelley and Sons Co.